What I've Learned Since I Knew It All is the kind of book I wish every incoming college freshman were required to read. It is a book I hope churches will give to their graduating seniors. While in college, Todd Clements was a leader in student government, in his fraternity, and in our ministry on campus. He and Paul Meier have written something they have lived.

This book is about real life and how to live it in a way that honors the Lord and makes the most of college years. This is a tool that will help both students and those who love them and work with them.

ARLISS DICKERSON
BAPTIST CAMPUS MINISTER, ARKANSAS STATE UNIVERSITY

This book is a must-read for everyone who is, has been, or is considering becoming a teenager! These two gifted psychiatrists sharing some of their life experiences makes not only an entertaining read but also a fantastic book on adolescent brain development. Drs. Clements and Meier wonderfully demonstrate how our brain functioning largely determines the type of person we become.

DANIEL G. AMEN, M.D.
CHILD, ADOLESCENT, AND ADULT PSYCHIATRIST
NEW YORK TIMES BEST-SELLING AUTHOR OF *CHANGE YOUR BRAIN CHANGE YOUR LIFE*

Practical, helpful, and engaging. Any former or current know-it-all will enjoy and benefit from *What I've Learned Since I Knew It All*. Dr. Todd Clements and Dr. Paul Meier wisely blend story and humor with insight toward a better life.

LINDA H. OSBORNE
NATIONAL COLLEGIATE MINISTRY LEADER FOR LIFEWAY CHRISTIAN RESOURCES,
SOUTHERN BAPTIST CONVENTION

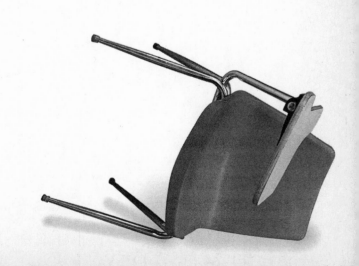

what
I've
since
i

12 SECRETS T

learned

I knew

all

ING A SATISFIED LIFE

PAUL MEIER, M.D.

TODD CLEMENTS, M.D.

Tyndale House Publishers, Inc.
CAROL STREAM, ILLINOIS

Visit Tyndale's exciting Web site at www.tyndale.com

TYNDALE and Tyndale's quill logo are registered trademarks of Tyndale House Publishers, Inc.

What I've Learned Since I Knew It All: 12 Secrets to Living a Satisfied Life

Designed by Ron Kaufmann

Published in association with the literary agency of Heidi Brizendine.

ISBN-13: 978-1-4143-1281-1

Printed in the United States of America

This book is dedicated to my parents,

Danny and Lou Anne Clements,

for their enduring love, patience, and wisdom

in dealing with this know-it-all.

TODD CLEMENTS, M.D.

CONTENTS

Know-It-Alls Don't Know It All

NOBODY WANTS TO BE labeled a know-it-all. Still, many people secretly believe they do have superior knowledge and intelligence, leading to the best decisions and wisest actions. They don't foresee any consequences to their actions or fallout from poor choices.

These attitudes, based on wishful thinking instead of reality, can result in near disaster, as in the case of one young man who once thought he had it all together.

He was twenty-one and honestly thought he knew it all—at least everything important to know. That year he had the highest grade point average of nearly five thousand students at his college. He was recently married and had accepted a hefty scholarship for a graduate program at a prestigious university. He used some of that cash to buy a brand-new Mercury Cougar—the latest model.

He was confident in his faith, having memorized hundreds of Bible verses and read his Bible daily since age ten. He was certain he'd have the right answer to any Bible question that could be fired in his direction. Yet a year later, at age twenty-two, this young man felt the urge to rebel. He dug into Bible prophecy and studied other religions—and almost ditched his Christian faith and his wife in the process. Thankfully, he eventually came to the conclusion that if he ditched Jesus, he would be ditching the truth, so he ruled that out as an option.

While in graduate school he attended a weekly "growth group." This was a new concept in the 1960s: Christians sitting around and confessing their faults to each other. After a few weeks in the group, one of the group members turned to the man who thought he knew it all and said, "I don't mean to offend you, but you are really defensive."

"I am not!" he retorted quickly.

One by one, five other group members said the same thing to this young man. He was sure they were mistaken. Still, he felt confused that so many people could be wrong at one time. As he and his wife walked to their Mercury Cougar after the meeting, he turned to her and blurted out, "Can you believe all those people think I am defensive when I am so extremely open?"

"I hate to say it, honey," she replied, "but I think you are too, in ways that you don't even realize."

And that was the first time it dawned on him clearly: *If six people in my group—and my own wife—all think I am defensive in some ways, then it must be theoretically possible that they could be right and I could be (theoretically speaking, of course) wrong.*

Day by day, God opened his eyes to the blind spots he had when it came to many of his personal failings.

He opened up in the group after that, and he grew up. He quit being a twelve-year-old know-it-all when he was twenty-two. By the time he was a psychiatry resident five years later, his professors said he was the most *defenseless* person they had ever met. He was willing and ready to admit anything that was true—even his own sinful thoughts.

When he started a national radio talk show, broadcasting daily to a million people, he was warned he wouldn't last long because he was too vulnerable. He was often willing to talk about his personal sins and failures in order to help other people be more open. He was occasionally taken off the air by certain stations for being too forthright, but most Christians appeared ready for a bout of honesty. It made people feel good to find out they weren't the only sinners trying to be good; even authority figures can have similar struggles and admit to being human.

Now, at age sixty, this man is confident in stating that the more he studies, the fewer things he really knows for certain.

The subject of that revealing story is actually one of the two authors of this book. I (Dr. Meier) admit I have made mistakes in my life, and I am thankful that today I'm being used by God as a psychiatrist who writes and speaks to hundreds of thousands of people, helping them solve problems and restore relationships. I was so thrilled when my wonderful friend Dr. Todd Clements asked if I would coauthor this book about what we've learned since we "knew it all." The title sounds like the story of my life. God isn't finished with me yet. I learn more of his love and grace and become more humble about my own ignorance every day, even at this ripe old age.

In this book you'll read some true stories about me (Dr. Clements) too. I also admit to once having known it all, but truly knowing better today.

While we are both recovering know-it-alls, we want to use our decades of counseling experience to help you reach that state sooner than we did.

Generally, becoming a know-it-all occurs in the teen years. Something strange happens during adolescence, and most teenagers become famous for insisting they are much smarter than their more-experienced, more-educated parents.

Sadly, many adolescents carry their know-it-all attitudes into adulthood, and a few even remain know-it-alls for their entire lives. These people or their family members often end up in psychiatrists' offices like ours—suffering deep emotional trauma due to their know-it-all attitudes.

Usually parents remember their own wayward days as young adults and their rebellious feelings toward their own parents, so they may let their teenagers' arrogant attitudes slide. But when teenage behavior continues into the midtwenties, serious interpersonal problems can erupt:

> Parents can become annoyed by an adult child who maintains an "I know better than you" attitude.
> Prospective employers are turned off by recent graduates and newcomers to a field who already deem themselves "experts."
> Romantic relationships can finally erode when one of the pair maintains a nonstop know-it-all attitude.

The teenage know-it-all faces many disadvantages, mostly due to his or her refusal to heed the warnings of parents who have been there before. Typically we adults remember shrugging off or laughing at our parents' advice, only to later discover how much misery and frustration we could have avoided if we had only listened in the first place.

Mark Twain once wrote, "When I was a boy of fourteen, my father was so ignorant I could hardly stand to have the old man around. But when I got to be twenty-one, I was astonished at how much the old man had learned in seven years."

Mark Twain is the pen name of the famous American author and sage Samuel Clemens. Because he was an astute observer of human behavior, his words will be found at the start of each chapter, helping to underscore each chapter's point.

Human nature remains the same today as it was one hundred years ago when Mark Twain made his observations. Young people are not likely to begin listening to their parents anytime soon. Maybe, however, they will listen to two self-proclaimed former know-it-alls who've learned from their mistakes and those of hundreds of counseling patients.

This book consists of twelve truths that we have learned since that time period when we knew it all. These twelve truths have made our lives better in countless ways. They have developed us into more thoughtful, caring, and loving human beings. They have helped us learn to get along with others and no doubt have allowed others to like us and enjoy being around us. They have helped us to become more successful in every life endeavor—largely due to the fact that every facet of life requires skills in dealing with other people.

These twelve truths have actually given us more self-confidence. Many know-it-alls feel insecure on the inside, so they overcompensate on the outside by portraying overconfidence. This is seen in the animal kingdom when some animals inhale to make themselves appear larger when facing a predator or stand up on their hind legs to look taller. We call it bluffing.

Walk by a yard that a poodle considers to be his territory and watch what happens. He starts with low-pitched growling and gets ready to pounce if you dare cross the sidewalk and touch one blade of his grass. He tries to make you think he's a people-eating poodle. But one lunge at the mutt reveals his true character: He backs up three steps and starts growling louder!

Today it's brains, rather than brawn, that dominate human society. People don't overcompensate with a show of force (except in war and psychiatric hospitals) but rather with an air of intelligence. They have an immediate answer for every situation. Mark Twain, too, had an immediate answer for everything, but his was slightly more humble: *"I was gratified to be able to answer promptly, and I did. I said I didn't know."*

It is when we arrive at this point and have the freedom to admit to ourselves and others that we don't know everything that we can finally be our authentic selves with no facades.

The Power of Authenticity

Dropping your facade allows you to connect with others. For the first time, you can actually feel their pain. You can enjoy their successes without jealousy and worry that others are "outdoing" you. You can truly celebrate life.

A know-it-all can only celebrate his own successes, but the authentic person can celebrate everyone's successes. Think how much more celebration this allows. The know-it-all usually pouts when others receive accolades or attention. The know-it-all can only celebrate a win by his football team if he had a good game and scored a touchdown; otherwise, the victory is bitter. An authentic person can revel in the victory, even if he never made it off the sideline the whole game!

Dropping the facade allows each of us to reveal our true identity to others. For the first time, others can actually feel and help comfort us in our pain. This aspect is difficult to grasp in today's society, especially among young males. We often believe that if others feel our pain or know our weaknesses, they will expose and open our wounds even more. People in emotional and physical pain often mask their loneliness and agony on the outside while secretly struggling within.

Have you ever smiled and calmly answered, "Just fine," when asked how life was treating you, meanwhile feeling on the verge of a nervous breakdown inside? We talk up all our victories and successes while hiding our pain in order to draw people to us, but in reality, shouldn't it be the other way around if we truly want the companionship and respect of others?

How much do you enjoy celebrating when a know-it-all succeeds? You might go to the party, but your celebration is most likely not sincere. Rarely does someone say, "I can't wait to hang out with so-and-so; all she does is talk about herself." Dropping the facade of being a know-it-all allows us to live in closer connection with others, which leads to a happier life.

The unhappiest people in the world are those who are not connected to others emotionally. Those who have no true friends have the highest rate of mental illness and are most likely to commit suicide.

Spend a weekend totally by yourself sometime and you will get a taste of this truth. If you have family at home, rent a motel room Friday night through Sunday. Spend those forty-eight hours without talking to any friends or family. By Monday morning you will be more than ready to go back to work, and you'll be nicer to everyone than you were on Friday.

Humans were made to bond with each other, and knowing-it-all negatively affects that bonding process.

Truth from the Source

The Bible, written two thousand years ago, addresses the subject of human nature, which was the same in ancient times as it is today.

Humanity's surroundings and technology change, but personalities remain the same. The Bible actually does more than merely identify and comment on human behavior. It teaches us how to improve it. The Bible does include lists of right and wrong, but it is much more than that. It shows us how to live as it examines relationships men and women had with each other and with God. We see examples of deplorable behavior, such as Judas Iscariot, who betrayed Jesus, and the Pharisees who excelled in know-it-all, holier-than-thou attitudes.

Righteous behavior is also depicted. We see Joseph run from sexual temptation when Potiphar's wife tries to entice him into bed with her. We then see how God rewards his faithfulness by putting Joseph in a position of leadership. The Bible depicts humans interacting with each other over a several-thousand-year time span. Through this dialogue we find truth.

The Bible supports the twelve truths we have learned. However, we both learned them the hard way.

Rather than taking the Bible at face value, I (Dr. Meier) tried calling the shots myself. When that no longer worked, I found the truth in two ways. With most of my wrong behaviors, I read the Bible and realized my error. With others, I simply tried doing things differently than I had been doing them before. I later found the solutions I discovered by this method were all supported by the Bible as well.

Throughout this book we have used various Bible passages and stories to help illustrate timeless truths. The Bible was written not only to teach us about God and His ways but also to guide us in living our lives during the short time we have been given upon this earth. We believe the Bible is just as relevant to our lives today as it was to the Jews two thousand years ago.

Ask yourself: How much impact does the Bible have in my daily life? Is it more than television or the Internet?

These twelve truths can help you avoid some of life's potholes and pitfalls. In addition to naming and titling each truth, we provide examples of how you can use these principles in your life. We also share personal events from our lives—and most of them illustrate the less-than-pretty results of ignoring these precepts.

As you read, try to remember some of your own life experiences. Write them down and we will let you know what to do with them at the end of the book.

This is probably the first book ever written where the goal is to come out looking less intelligent than you did before you started.

CHAPTER 1

One Person Can Make a Difference

So Share Your Convictions

*The longer I live, the clearer I perceive how unmatchable,
how unapproachable a compliment one pays when he says
of a man "he has the courage to utter his convictions."*

MARK TWAIN IN A LETTER TO W. D. HOWELLS

FEBRUARY 15, 1887

◆

*An honest man in politics shines more
there than he would elsewhere.*

MARK TWAIN, *A TRAMP ABROAD*

"I'M SO TICKED OFF about this election!" ranted Melody, a nineteen-year-old college freshman sitting on my (Dr. Clements) office couch. "Everyone I was for—from president to congressman, down to mayor of my town—lost. What's worse is now I have to listen to my parents and preppy brother, who were staunch supporters of the other party, celebrate."

As we talked, I learned that Melody chose to support a certain political party because of one issue she felt very strongly about. She repeatedly commented on how this belief she held so dearly was now going to be outlawed, which would wind up hurting thousands of people.

"I've worked hard for campaigns I strongly believed in and have lost. It's tough," I said, trying to reassure her.

"Well, I really didn't do any work for the campaign," Melody sheepishly admitted.

"But you supported those people and voted for them," I said.

"Well, I actually didn't even vote this time," she said.

"Why not?"

"My sorority was building a float that day for the homecoming parade the next weekend. Plus I knew the guys I supported didn't have a chance of winning anyway. My vote would not have changed the outcome."

"Did anybody in your sorority vote?" I asked.

"I doubt it." Melody shrugged her shoulders.

"Did you tell anyone in your sorority how you feel about these political issues?"

"No, we don't talk about stuff like that," she said impatiently.

"Did you tell anyone else?" I kept probing.

"No, who's going to listen to a college freshman?" she shot back.

"I can see now why you are frustrated, Melody. You spent a whole week working hard to let people know you had pride and cared about your school's football team, which probably didn't make any difference in the game, but you never shared with anybody key issues in your life that *could* have made a difference."

The truth is that one vote rarely makes a difference in an election, but one person does. One voice making a complaint rarely changes things, but one person does. How? When one person uses his or her one voice, another voice soon joins in, and then another and another. Those other voices continue adding even more voices, until the message is too loud to ignore.

Christianity was started by one man, Jesus, whose message was carried on by a handful of disciples who had neither wealth nor stature in the world. Today, more than 2.1 billion people follow Christ's teachings.

Three Keys to Success

One person can do amazing things, but that person must possess three key elements: determination, work, and time.

> *Determination.* Whatever you stand for, you will encounter naysayers. In the early 1900s, people told Orville and Wilbur Wright that they were downright stupid for thinking they could make a machine that would fly. Experts said there were no motors powerful enough to sustain a "flying machine," and even if there were, it would be impossible to steer it correctly. Several other inventors in Great Britain had tried to make flying machines, but sadly, some of them had died when their experimental crafts crashed. Americans laughed at those two brothers from Dayton, Ohio, who worked on their flying machine for three years. The pair continued to believe it could be done, and in 1903 they showed everyone when they successfully flew a plane on the seashore at Kitty Hawk, North Carolina.

> *Work.* Thomas Edison, a man who was largely deaf and had only three months of formal education, is credited with more inventions than any other American (over 1,300). Edison certainly knew how to work. He created the phonograph machine, the movie camera, the battery, and even an electric vote recorder in 1868. Though he was a genius, his achievements didn't come easily. In fact, it was Thomas Edison who made the now-famous statement "Genius is one percent inspiration and 99 percent perspiration." Whenever he set his mind to invent something, he spent months reading every piece of literature he could obtain about the subject.

In 1878, even though he was already wealthy and could have retired, Edison became convinced that electric lights would be cheaper for people and more efficient than gas lighting. Although electricity was very crude at the time, he was convinced he could find a substance from which he could make a "filament" that would transmit electric energy into light.

He tried thousands of different substances over the next several months, but each one failed. The entire time he worked, the *New York Times* and the gas industry lampooned him. But he did not give up or waver, and finally, after months of failure, he created a carbon filament that would glow for hours when electricity was run through it. It was the first light bulb, and it changed the world. What would life be like today if he had given up?

> *Time.* If you are consistent over time, people will listen. Dr. Robert Atkins came up with an idea over a quarter of a century ago that overweight people could lose pounds by eating low levels of carbohydrates and higher levels of protein and fat in their diet. This idea was the opposite of what the government and the American Medical Association (AMA) were telling people to do to lose weight. The AMA endorsed low fat and low protein diets.

Dr. Atkins could have said, "Who am I to go up against all these other powerful doctors who say my method is crazy?" But he didn't. He kept preaching and teaching his conviction that this diet was an effective and safe way to lose weight. He had very few listeners for the first several years.

A recent magazine article reported that one out of every seven people in America today follow an Atkins-type diet. Restaurants have even started changing their menus to include low carbohydrate foods. Soft drink and beer companies have created new drinks with fewer carbohydrates. Grocery stores now carry foods labeled "Atkins Approved." This craze is not only in America but in other countries as well. One man's ideas have affected the eating habits of millions of people.

We are not trying to say that the Atkins diet is the best way to lose weight, because we both believe in permanent lifestyle changes when it comes to eating correctly. But a modified Atkins approach, with some healthy carbohydrates from fruits and vegetables, *can* add years to some people's lives by helping them lose weight. Dr. Atkins accomplished a lot and taught a great deal about nutrition by continuing to speak about his conviction.

New ideas are often controversial. The Atkins method certainly falls into that category. There was also controversy when the Wright brothers talked about flying machines, and when Thomas Edison said electric lights would be better than gas lighting. Any matter of consequence in life is going to be accompanied by controversy. If it doesn't, it means no one really cares. Controversy or the lack of instant success should never stop you from proclaiming your convictions.

Do you want to make a difference in this world? We've got good news—you can do it! And you have an even better chance at success if you determine and start working for your convictions while you are young.

Stand Up for Your Convictions

How strongly do you feel about your convictions? Do you feel strongly enough to vote? On Election Day 2004, it rained all day in the state of Ohio. Thousands of concerned citizens, including many Amish Christians, who normally stay out of politics, lined up in the rain to vote. The lines were so long because so many people that year wanted to voice their moral convictions about key issues such as partial-birth abortion, gay marriage, and religious rights. Many had to leave the voting lines and go to work without having voted. But after working an eight- to twelve-hour day, they returned to the voting lines, with it still raining. Some Ohio citizens did not get to vote until two in the morning. We consider these people to be heroes, no matter how they voted. They had the courage and moral character to withstand extreme discomfort in order to vote their convictions.

Are *you* going to vote in future elections? Are *you* going to volunteer your time working for the candidates and ideas you believe in? Do you have the courage to defend the genuine civil liberties of evangelical believers?

There are so many ways for one person to make a difference. By voting, and persuading others to vote as well, your single vote carries much more weight. Consider the ripple effect of one person's efforts. You might influence six or seven people, who then go on to influence six or seven more people each. Eventually, your single influence might reach hundreds of thousands or even millions of people. A few million fired-up college students could have the power to sway almost every election in their favor.

Remember Melody? She claimed she never shared her convictions because no one would listen to a college student. Well a sixty-year-old might not, but other college students would probably be willing to listen. Start with your peers. There is a misperception in our country that wealthy, influential people have all the say-so, and the rest of us have to go along with their plans. Nothing could be further from the truth.

Live by Your Convictions

▶ *Paul Meier*

I used to attend church in a town with several restaurants in which church members dined regularly. Some of these restaurants advertised in a small independent newspaper, a publication that featured a few news stories but mainly served to promote the city's "gentlemen's (strip) clubs" and to hook gay men and lesbian women up with dates. The paper was free, so its only source of revenue was its advertisers.

A young couple felt convicted that by dining at the restaurants that advertised, they were indirectly supporting the paper. The young husband and wife visited with the restaurant managers and were largely shunned when they voiced their concern. They spoke with the pastor about the matter, and he agreed with their conviction.

He allowed the couple to address the congregation on Sunday morning and tell the church members they had decided not to dine in any of the restaurants that continued supporting this newspaper. The husband said, "It will be hard because we both love the food and atmosphere in several of these places, but our convictions are more important, and we are determined to follow them before pleasure." They passed around a sign-up sheet welcoming others to join their cause, but asked only those who were determined to follow through with the boycott to sign up.

Several hundred people signed the list. The couple then went back to the restaurant managers—and even some owners this time—and asked if they wanted to see the list. Most of the managers said no and were even ruder this time. As church members told their friends and family about the situation, the boycott grew bigger and bigger. Soon the issue ignited a firestorm. Restaurant employees admitted that within a week business had gone from crowds waiting for a table to rooms nearly empty of customers.

The gay and lesbian community took the boycott issue to the press and tried to portray the church members as people who were spreading hate against their lifestyle. The young couple who started the boycott were very eloquent when interviewed, explaining how they had politely shared their convictions with the restaurant managers, who in turn were rude and condescending to them.

The wife said, "Hey, we just decided there are many other great restaurants in this city with wonderful food in which we can spend our money. It just so happens that several thousand of our friends decided to do the same as well."

Needless to say, within a month the restaurants dropped the ads and decided not to distribute the paper at their businesses. Because of the media coverage garnered by the homosexual community, many other advertisers pulled out as well. The newspaper soon went out of production. One couple had sparked thousands to live out their convictions and changed a whole city.

It would be nice to say that all was happy ever after, but that's not the whole story. This young couple faced harassment from people sympathetic to the now-defunct paper. Sadly, this is the way society often works. Rather than spending their time and energy looking for new businesses or individuals to support the newspaper, which would have produced much more successful results, the owners wanted a scapegoat on which to blame the paper's failure. The young couple bravely stood firm while enduring harassment. Once the opposition realized they were having little or no effect on the couple, they gave up.

This young couple is now well respected in their community. Community leaders want the husband to run for political office, which he probably will do in the next few years. People know that when he believes in something, he will stand up for it. He is already a proven leader. Although the opposition had threatened to destroy his reputation and his business, his business has actually quadrupled since the boycott.

Thankfully he had a clean reputation, because these groups dug deep for dirt on him but couldn't find anything. He had married his college sweetheart, didn't run around on her, and never had any trouble with the law. Opponents even combed the strip club's records going back several years to see if he

*had ever been to one of them. They tried every means pos-
sible to make him look like a hypocrite.*

We cannot emphasize this point enough. If you want to make a difference in life—if you want people to listen to, understand, and adopt
your convictions, you must live by them and be willing to start making
a difference.

As the couple in the story above found, living by your convictions
also means keeping your record clean. A woman we know spent several
years teaching school and found her convictions at odds with the sexual
education classes. The curriculum was taught by her state's so-called
experts. She spoke with the state education board several times about
adding sexual abstinence as a valid option for avoiding unwanted teen
pregnancy, AIDS, and a host of other sexually transmitted diseases.
The "experts" said this was a silly option and a waste of time because
students could not and would not take it seriously. Instead they were
aiming at safe sex methods and condoning free birth control and con-
dom machines in school.

This woman stopped teaching, but with a continued large heart for
adolescents she began meeting with a few students from her former
school (off school grounds and not during school hours). These high
school students started an abstinence group in which each member
committed to sexual abstinence until he or she was married. The group
started small but steadily grew. Soon the woman was asked to form new
groups at other nearby high schools, which she did, on her own time
and at her own expense, apart from school hours.

A few years later, a group of citizens persuaded the state legislature
to sponsor a bill including abstinence as an alternative in sex education classes in the public schools. The American Civil Liberties Union
(ACLU) fought hard against this bill, and the matter was finally brought
to a hearing before a state legislative subcommittee.

The day of the hearing found a room packed with area high school
students who belonged to some of the abstinence groups started by the

former teacher. Several ACLU lawyers also came to argue before the committee. The former teacher was allowed to speak first. She simply said, "I want to introduce you to some high school students who have made important decisions about their lives."

One by one, dozens of students walked to the podium and described how they had pledged sexual abstinence until marriage. The students were articulate, and every person in the room could hear the determination in their voices. When the last student finished, an ACLU lawyer began to describe how ludicrous it was to expect high school students to take abstinence seriously.

But it was clear that the kids had made his argument irrelevant before he ever spoke a word. They did all of this by simply having the courage to stand up and speak from their convictions.

Abstinence was incorporated into the school curriculum because one woman was convinced the "experts" were wrong and possessed the determination and work ethic to prove it. And abstinence is now taught in many nations of the world with great success.

Many adolescents never consider that their conduct today affects their future. But if you think what you do today won't have any bearing on your life thirty years down the road, you are wrong.

When you stand up for something you believe in, you may find people sifting through your history with a fine-tooth comb to expose any blemish. Written or computer records exist for almost any transaction today, so background checks are easy. Half of the places we go now are recorded by camera. Phone records can be gathered in an instant.

Look at the research political groups perform on rival candidates during an election year. They can produce a picture of a candidate attending an obscure meeting more than thirty years ago. In the future, it is possible someone will be able to tell you every Internet site you have looked at or phone call you have made. Romans 12:17 reminds us: "Be careful to do what is right in the eyes of everybody."

▶ *Todd Clements*

My father used to take me deer hunting annually. I looked forward to that November weekend for the whole year. I usually got to miss school on Friday and hunt during the weekend. The deer camp was two hours from my house and located on an island in the Mississippi River. Being there was like going back in time; we had no running water and no electricity except what we got from a small generator. There were about twenty people that stayed in our camp, ranging from old men to kids my age.

I hunted by myself when I was in the seventh grade. Even though we were on an island with several roads running through it, there was still the possibility of getting lost, especially after dark.

One of the old-timers in the camp used to tell us kids each year that if we ever got lost, we should find a nearby tree stump, stand up on it, and pull down our pants. Some kid who was new to the camp would inevitably give a puzzled look and ask, "Why?"

The old-timer would answer very seriously, "Because somebody will see you."

We all knew he was joking, even though he tried to act serious about this advice.

Even though the old-timer was kidding, you can understand his point. If you're doing something you know you shouldn't, watch out, because somebody will notice. This is especially true when you're doing something wrong. It may be easy to think no one notices because nobody confronts you about it, but often people do notice and tell other people instead.

Whether or not others notice, God sees everything we do. How would our behavior change if we never forgot about that fact? Romans 14:12 says: "So then, each of us will give an account of himself to God." This shouldn't scare you but rather encourage you to live as God wants you to. No one in the history of the world has ever been perfect except for Jesus. God doesn't expect you to be perfect—if He did, there would have been no need for Jesus to come to earth and die on the cross. Intelligent people realize that everyone makes mistakes. The Bible tells us that we all fail in many ways. However, if you don't live out the convictions you profess, you can actually do more harm for your cause than good.

What if one of the students from the abstinence group had had sex with his girlfriend in spite of promising he would abstain until marriage? What impact would it have had if the ACLU lawyer had then had the girlfriend testify to the subcommittee? It would have confirmed his argument that high school students can't take abstinence seriously. That might have been enough to keep abstinence from being taught in schools.

People who profess to believe one way while living another are called hypocrites. When Jesus was on the earth, the people he had the most problems with and spoke most harshly to were the arrogant, hypocritical religious leaders. You can be a "religious," legalistic, controlling, and arrogant hypocrite too if you want to be. This is a free country, after all. But when you get old and look back on your life, what do you want to see?

One word of caution: When you begin speaking about your convictions, many times other people who don't share those convictions will accuse you of judging them. If they know you are a Christian they will often throw Matthew 7:1-2 at you:

> **Do not judge, or you too will be judged. For in the same way you judge others, you will be judged, and with the measure you use, it will be measured to you.**

But if you read further in that chapter to verse 5, you'll realize that Jesus is talking about hypocrites here. If you speak of a conviction that you are living by, you are not judging others. You are simply saying, "Here's what I believe, and this is how I live." You are not telling others what to do. When the abstinence group testified, they never said other methods of "safe sex" should not be taught; they simply asked that their method be given a voice as well. It was actually the ACLU lawyers who were judging, saying that abstinence did not deserve to be mentioned to high school students as a way to prevent unwanted pregnancies and diseases.

The Bottom Line

We all get one life on this earth. And with determination, work, and time, one person can make a very big difference. Are you determined to use your life to make a difference, no matter what the cost? You can do it! Begin by deciding what your convictions are. Then, with God's help, live out those convictions and speak out to others about them.

CHAPTER 2

Life Is Not Fair

So Use What You've Been Given

*We recognize that there are no trivial occurrences
in life if we get the right focus on them.*

MARK TWAIN'S AUTOBIOGRAPHY

✦

*There was never yet an uninteresting life. Such
a thing is an impossibility. Inside of the dullest
exterior there is a drama, a comedy, and a tragedy.*

MARK TWAIN, "THE REFUGE OF DERELICTS," 1905

WHEN I (DR. CLEMENTS) WAS A SENIOR in high school, the football season started out great. We had an awesome quarterback who could throw the ball almost directly into my hands. He and I were good friends and had practiced together so much that catching balls from him became natural. In the fourth game of the season, we were tied 0–0 during the fourth quarter. James, the quarterback, soared a pass that I had to jump up to catch. I held on to the ball and even stayed on my feet as I dropped back down to earth. I saw an opening down the sidelines and ran that way, heading toward the end zone.

I was nearly there when I felt somebody grab me from the back. I stretched out to place the ball over the goal line and *whack!* I hit the ground about one foot short. The next play was a successful quarterback sneak, thanks to our team's center, a guy who weighed over 300 pounds. Jumping up, running for the sideline to put on my kicking shoe for the extra point, I felt a sharp pain in my ankle. *The pain will go away in a minute,* I told myself and went on with the game. The extra point bounced off some guy's head, and my ankle continued throbbing.

Now I had a new problem! I was the kickoff man. What should I do? We were up 6–0 with a few minutes left. Should I kick off lame and risk ruining our lead?

I motioned for the coach to bring someone else out to kick off, but he just motioned back for me to kick it. The kickoff went okay, but the other team's receiver broke through our line and came at me! I hobbled up and grabbed hold, slowing him down just enough for the defense to catch him. I then limped to the sidelines with no idea that I had just played my last ever game of football.

I was able to walk that night (though in considerable pain) and enjoy our victory dinner. The next morning, however, my foot looked like a gourd. A trip to the emergency room was reassuring. "Only a sprain," the doctor said. "Rest on it until Wednesday; then start walking. You might miss next week's game, but that should be all."

Tuesday brought an unexpected twist. A radiologist from the hospital called and told my parents that I was not to walk on my ankle at all. He had performed a final reading on all the weekend X-rays and discovered that my ankle was badly broken. He had already scheduled an appointment with the orthopedic doctor for the next day.

Wednesday changed my life. We learned that not only was my ankle broken, but the bones were displaced and I would need surgery to receive titanium pins. I would be on crutches for three months. Football was over and basketball probably was too.

I was devastated. How could God do this to me? What would I do with the rest of my life now? Would my girlfriend put up with carting around a cripple?

What happened next? Am I still heartbroken over this loss? You might not believe this, but that broken ankle was the best thing that had ever happened in my life up to that point! My broken ankle taught me I wasn't invincible. Sitting home with free time on my hands for the first time in years, I started reading the Bible and realized my need for God.

My injury allowed me to realize *who* I was for the first time and not *what* I was (a football player). It spared me from going to a small college that I did not really want to attend just to play football. Instead I went to a larger college with my friends, loved every minute of it, and became involved with the purposes God had for me. Every time I think about that whole event, the apostle Paul's words in Romans ring true: "And we know that in all things God works for the good of those who love him, who have been called according to his purpose" (Romans 8:28).

Individual Gifts

Dr. Clements thought he was gifted as a football player. But that didn't turn out to be the most important gift in his life.

What about you? God has endowed you with certain gifts and talents. Your gifts are different from our gifts; they are different from your best friend's gifts. In order to live life to the fullest you must exercise and improve your gifts and stay open to the possibility that they will change in the future. It may seem like unfairness at the time, but the whole truth will eventually become clear.

Instead of exercising their unique gifts, people sometimes start looking at other people's gifts and comparing themselves. Soon they find someone who has something they don't and they start envying that gift, spending time and energy to obtain it. This takes them away from their own gifts.

The apostle Paul warned us in Galatians 6 not to compare ourselves with other people. Instead, we are instructed to compare ourselves with how we used to be in the past and to be proud of ourselves for the progress we are making.

Between the two of us, Dr. Meier has the "gift of gab." He can talk to a squirrel and make it feel comfortable. Dr. Clements is also warm and friendly, but his gift is that of a "Mark Twain–like brain." He is like a walking encyclopedia.

On the national radio talk show that we do together (called *The Meier Clinic*), we make a great combination. Dr. Meier puts the nervous callers at ease and provides good advice, and then Dr. Clements remembers the latest research on the topic and exactly how to address it. We are not jealous of one another's gifts, but instead we appreciate them and use them together to serve God and help people lessen their pain.

▶ Todd Clements

My two best friends, Kent Keith and Mickey Ryan, both have natural talents that I don't. Kent is very funny and can remember every joke he's heard. He knows the right comeback for every situation. Once in college a large group of us went to a comedy club. In between acts Kent jumped up onstage and started telling jokes and heckling the crowd. The whole place was in stitches. The upcoming comedian finally had him kicked off the stage! I envied that to the point where I started trying to memorize jokes. But it was painful for my friends who had to listen to me try to tell jokes. I quickly realized the talent is not in remembering the jokes but in the timing and the way they are told.

Mickey has the uncanny ability to remember the name of everyone he meets. In addition he can give a thirty-minute impromptu speech on any subject—whether he knows about it or not. I wanted this talent for myself so much that I started trying to recall the name of everyone I met. This led to me calling Bob by the name of Jerry and yelling, "Hey, Susan," at Casey. I did get better at remembering names, but I never reached Mickey's level of expertise.

I never could do a thirty-minute impromptu speech and still can't. On the other hand, Dr. Meier does almost everything off the cuff. You could wake him up at three in the morning, put a microphone in front of him, and tell him to give a speech to the whole world on almost any topic, and he would just begin sharing whatever he knows about that subject without batting an eye. When he is invited to preach a sermon (he is a psychiatrist, but we both have seminary training as well), he often waits until he hears the special song right before his sermon, then gets up and delivers a forty-minute message on whatever the song was about. It is a gift I will never have. But if you ask Kent or Mickey or Dr. Meier, I guarantee they'll tell you about natural talents that I have which they don't.

In seventh grade I tried out for quarterback of the football team. I would have made a good quarterback except for one problem—I couldn't throw. I spent that year and the next trying to throw the ball and playing in positions that did not fit my talent range. It wasn't until I finally accepted I wasn't going to be quarterback that I finally excelled.

Guess what? I realized I did have a talent. Catching! When I began focusing on receiving, I excelled.

God didn't design everyone to be a great quarterback. Dr. Meier tells me he loves sports dearly, but he is so uncoordinated he can't walk and chew gum at the same time. Though president of his college fraternity, six-foot-four Dr. Meier still got cut from their basketball team. They let him be on the fraternity baseball team to warm up the bench and cheer on the other players, but he never even got into a single game. Yet he is the type of guy who was happy just to be part of a team and to inspire everyone to do better.

When Life Seems Unfair

God has not left you all alone in the ocean of life without support. He has given you specific gifts and talents. He also uses events in your life to mold you. He makes lemonade out of lemons, and we must look for the lemonade rather than focus on the lemons.

▶ *Paul Meier*

I grew up financially poor and had to work to buy my own clothes starting at age thirteen.

My mom was a maid and had only gone to school until the third grade. My dad was a carpenter who didn't make very much money. I wanted to be a carpenter like my dad, but when I was sixteen, God gave me two very vivid dreams that changed all that.

In the first dream, God told me he wanted me to become a doctor. I woke up, immediately kneeled beside my bed, and said yes. Then I went back to sleep. Later that same night I dreamed I was a middle-aged man going from country to country sharing practical truths that greatly benefited the lives of those who heard me speak.

After that dream, I started taking college prep courses and studied hard to become a doctor. Once I received my medical degree, I trained to become a psychiatrist and then a theologian. When I finished my psychiatry residency at Duke University in 1975, I was offered a psychiatry job with a great salary. I remember praying, Thank you, God, for calling me into psychiatry!

But God showed me that I could do more good by training pastors to be excellent counselors than by simply being a psychiatric counselor myself. So I turned down the lucrative job and taught full-time at Dallas Theological Seminary for the next twelve years. I had a part-time psychiatric practice on the side, but my wife and I still barely survived financially.

There weren't any textbooks on Christian psychology available in 1975, so I wrote one for each course I taught. This was an outgrowth of my gift of gab. I wrote Happiness Is a Choice *in two weeks during Christmas break. I also wrote a few novels, some of them in one week. When it flows, it flows. I ended up writing more than seventy books; some (such as* Love Is a Choice*) sold over a million copies.*

I went from a life of poverty to life as a millionaire. I saw this as God blessing me for making the tough decisions earlier. But the money went to my head. I started buying condominiums in Padre Island and in Colorado and spent too much time thinking about money and paying the bills on those places. I foolishly trusted all of my money to a "Christian investor," and in the end, I lost everything financially.

It was the best thing that ever happened to me. Losing all my money helped me to get my life in perspective again, to realize that my purpose is to love and be loved just as Jesus does. I lost all my clinics, but I eventually got them back and turned them into a nonprofit organization. Now we provide over a million dollars a year in charitable care to about 3,400 clients who could not afford therapy otherwise.

My wife and I own a nice house in a blue-collar area of Garland, Texas, and a 1994 BMW. Other than that, I don't own anything else and don't even want to. I have the best job in the world, even fulfilling my second dream by traveling all over the world to teach people practical Christian psychology. Over a million people have chosen to follow Christ as a result of the various Meier Clinic ministries.

I've had the privilege of witnessing great successes by my students also. When I moved to Dallas in the 1970s, one of my first students was Tony Evans, a young man who was so outstanding that I took him to lunch almost every Thursday for three years. He is now a leading pastor in America, ministering to people around the world through books, radio, and his Urban Renewal projects.

Other students that I've been able to disciple include authors John Townsend, Henry Cloud, John Trent, Graham Barker, Abede Alexandre, and many more. It has been so personally satisfying to see them use their lives to positively change the lives of other people for the better.

So now we want to ask you a personal question. What bad events has God used in your life to define and refine you? Are you allowing him to refine you?

At the time, it seemed unfair when Dr. Clements lost his ability to play football. The truth is, life is frequently unfair to each of us. If your parents didn't teach you that concept early in life, you're in for a rude awakening. Bad things happen to good people. Good things happen to bad people. Children die and innocent people are killed.

Some people believe that bad things in life are the result of specific sins. That's not necessarily true. Jesus addressed this in the story of the man born blind:

> **As He passed by, He saw a man blind from birth. And His disciples asked Him, "Rabbi, who sinned, this man or his parents,**

that he would be born blind?" Jesus answered, "It was neither that this man sinned, nor his parents; but it was so that the works of God might be displayed in him."   JOHN 9:1-3, NASB

Jesus spoke to this situation again in the story of the tower collapse in Siloam:

Those eighteen who died when the tower in Siloam fell on them—do you think they were more guilty than all the others living in Jerusalem? I tell you, no! But unless you repent, you too will all perish.   LUKE 13:4-5

The wicked do actually prosper at times. This reality flabbergasted King David, who complained often to God in his prayers (as recorded throughout the book of Psalms) about how angry he was that God allowed the unjust to prosper sometimes.

There is an old saying, "Life is 10 percent how you make it and 90 percent how you take it." We say it this way: "You must know how to take life before you can make life." God can make blessings out of our beatings, but we must be willing.

Look at some of the statements the apostle Paul makes in Philippians:

> I always pray with joy.   —PHILIPPIANS 1:4
> Christ is preached. And because of this I rejoice. Yes, and I will continue to rejoice.   —PHILIPPIANS 1:18
> For to me, to live is Christ and to die is gain.   —PHILIPPIANS 1:21
> Do everything without complaining or arguing.
> —PHILIPPIANS 2:14
> I am glad and rejoice with all of you.   —PHILIPPIANS 2:17
> Finally, my brothers, rejoice in the Lord! It is no trouble for me to write the same things to you again, and it is a safeguard for you.
> —PHILIPPIANS 3:1

> Rejoice in the Lord always. I will say it again: Rejoice!
>   —PHILIPPIANS 4:4

> I rejoice greatly in the Lord that at last you have renewed your
> concern for me.   —PHILIPPIANS 4:10

> For I have learned to be content whatever the circumstances.
>   —PHILIPPIANS 4:11

> I know what it is to be in need, and I know what it is to have
> plenty. I have learned the secret of being content in any and every
> situation, whether well fed or hungry, whether living in plenty or
> in want.   —PHILIPPIANS 4:12

> I can do everything through him who gives me strength.
>   —PHILIPPIANS 4:13

What was going on in Paul's life when he wrote this letter? It sounds as
if he had just won a million dollars.

Hardly! Look at the last part of verse 13 in the first chapter: "I am in
chains for Christ" (Philippians 1:13). Paul was in prison when he wrote
this! Could you be that excited about life if you were chained up with
no idea if you would ever be set free?

Circumstances cannot bring us contentment. After the apostle
Paul dedicated his life to Christ, he was shipwrecked several times,
nearly stoned to death, and imprisoned. Many times, he went without
food, and ultimately, he was killed for being a Christian. When we get
to heaven and ask, "Hey Paul, was life fair?" surely he will reply, "Not at
all. I didn't deserve to be called by God to share in his sufferings. What
a privileged life I had, to be able to write some of the books of the Bible
and to suffer for Jesus and eventually die for him. No, life was not fair. I
did not deserve all those awesome opportunities."

Real Gifts

The person who's always wondering if life is fair misses life by focusing
on circumstances. The highest suicide rates are actually found among
the wealthiest segments of the population. We see wealthy people in our

practices who complain that life's not worth living. It would be easy to say to them, "Hey, why don't we trade places? I think I can continue to be happy in your huge house on the lake and driving your sports car that will do 180 mph. I know you won't have any problem being miserable in my apartment or driving my truck."

Is it wrong to have material things? No, not at all. But if you are counting on these things to make you happy, you will surely be disappointed. Money doesn't guarantee happiness; it simply buys more lawsuits, more bills, more repairs, more problems, and more superficial friends to take advantage of you. If you find your self-worth in your net worth, you are in big trouble.

A reporter asked John D. Rockefeller, the richest man on earth, "Sir, how much money is enough?" John D. scratched his chin and then answered her honestly and bluntly, "Just a little bit more."

The book of Ecclesiastes tells us that if God blesses us with great wealth, we should enjoy it and thank him for it, but we shouldn't live for it. The meaning of life is to love God with all our souls and to love our neighbors as ourselves. This kind of biblical love is the only thing worth living for. And God has gifted each one of us to do that in our own way.

What if you have no idea what your gifts and abilities are? You must spend some time with God in order to discover them. Those who know you best, such as family members and close friends, can help as well. Sometimes you just have to step out and take some chances before God gives you answers.

But some people waste their lives sitting around waiting for the perfect time, trying to realize and fulfill *what* they are (football player, cheerleader, girlfriend, boyfriend, valedictorian, class clown, future rock star) rather than focusing on what's most important: knowing *who* they are.

▶ *Paul Meier*

I wanted to be a carpenter. There was nothing wrong with that if that was also what God wanted me to be. I would have been a good and honest carpenter, and perhaps even persuaded my dad to go into business with me to build houses. As a young teen, I had designed a house that my dad actually liked enough to build. We lived in that house a few years before selling it for a nice profit.

But God didn't want me to be a carpenter. First and foremost, he wanted me to be a committed follower of him. And once I realized who he wanted me to be, I was better able to discern his direction regarding what he wanted me to be. He wanted me to be a psychiatrist who could help people to understand mental illnesses. I would rather be who God called me be than to be president of the United States or even the king of the world.

Answering this one question will make all the difference: Who does God want me to be? We live but one life on this earth. Every day lost is one you can't get back. Live it to the fullest.

The Bottom Line

God has instilled in each of us unique gifts and abilities, and he uses our life experiences to improve those gifts and abilities. When we exercise and refine our abilities, we will live joyful, productive, and purpose-filled lives. But coveting others' gifts or circumstances takes our focus off our own design and leads to a life of disappointment and bitterness rather than fulfillment and joy.

Life is not fair. Thank God! If it were, we'd have to be as miserable as everyone else is. Wonderfully, God teaches us how to be joyful in all situations.

> **Only one life, 'twill soon be past. Only what's done for Christ will last.**
>
> *From a hymn by Charles Thomas Studd, missionary to Africa*

CHAPTER 3

Honesty Is the Best Policy

So Stop Trying to Justify Your Actions

You ought to never "sass" old people—unless they "sass" you first.

MARK TWAIN, *ADVICE FOR GOOD LITTLE GIRLS*

ARE YOU OLD ENOUGH to remember the O. J. Simpson double murder case from the 1990s? One of the key players in that famous trial was Mark Fuhrman, a Los Angeles Police Department detective. Simpson's defense lawyers painted Mr. Fuhrman as a racist. Though Detective Fuhrman vehemently denied these accusations, the defense produced an audiotape of Fuhrman clearly speaking in an obviously racist manner. This tape served to nullify his credibility and damage his testimony against O. J. Simpson. Many who still believe Simpson was guilty of the murders of his ex-wife and her boyfriend point to Mark Fuhrman as the primary reason he was acquitted.

Several months after the trial, Mark Fuhrman was interviewed on national television. The interviewer asked him point-blank whether he considered himself to be a racist, a liar, or both. His answer—shockingly—was "none of the above." He beat around the bush, focused on technicalities, and explained that he hadn't really lied and was never really a racist.

An informed person watching this interview might ask, "How can Fuhrman sit there and say he's not a racist and a liar? We heard the tape. Is he crazy?"

Actually, no, he's not crazy. He's very normal; his mind was doing what everyone's mind does every day. We are all very good at finding ways to justify our behaviors, and this practice of self-deception is described in detail in the Bible.

Honesty with God

Nearly three thousand years ago the prophet Jeremiah taught about the human heart, referring to the emotional heart that contains a person's innermost thoughts, feelings, and motives. According to Jeremiah, this heart is more deceptive (even self-deceiving) than anything else God created in his universe. Jeremiah asked the rhetorical question, "Who can understand it?" (Jeremiah 17:9).

David even asked God to reveal his innermost thoughts because he wanted to walk on a path that was pleasing to God (Psalm 139:23-24). In Hebrews, we are taught to meditate on Scripture because of our self-deceit (Hebrews 4:12-13, KJV). The author says that the Word of God is quick and powerful and able to reveal to us our innermost thoughts.

In order to become psychiatrists, we (Dr. Clements and Dr. Meier) had to complete college, medical school, internships, and psychiatry residencies. Throughout the course of our training, we learned a lot about defense mechanisms—the many ways that people lie to themselves. At least forty different defense mechanisms have been identified.

When we assess a new client, our job is to make an educated guess about what is truly going on in that person's brain—spiritually, emotionally, hormonally, and biochemically. We study the client's body language as well as his or her words and tone of voice. We commonly ask questions about emotions such as "Are you angry at your father for being too busy to spend time with you?"

The client may exhibit tear-filled eyes and a reddening neck and face, and might answer in a loud voice, "No, of course not! I'm not angry!" But these clients are not lying to us; they are only lying to themselves. Through therapy, we gently strip people of their defense mechanisms, guiding them to face the truth. The truth hurts and brings many tears, but the truth also sets us free from self-deception.

The Bible addresses the dangers of self-deceptive thinking: "There is a way that seems right to a man, but in the end it leads to death" (Proverbs 14:12).

King Solomon, the wisest man ever to live, wrote this because he knew how our minds allow us to overlook our own evil actions. As a young man Solomon asked God for wisdom, and God granted Solomon's request. Ultimately that great wisdom led to massive wealth. King Solomon studied with the best teachers and was skilled in language, science, and architecture. Solomon built magnificent palaces and buildings. But as wise as Solomon was, he still made many foolish choices that went against the will of God. Near the end of his life he wrote the book of Ecclesiastes and affirmed that living life outside of God's plan is utterly meaningless.

So if Solomon, the wisest man who ever lived, could justify his evil behaviors, how can we avoid doing the same? The first step in facing reality involves being honest with ourselves. We need to be humble enough to recognize that everything we think and feel and believe is just a guess our brains have made. Some of our guesses are correct. Many of them are wrong. We cannot trust our own judgment.

As I (Dr. Meier) mentioned before, when I was sixteen years old, I planned to be a carpenter like my dad. But one Sunday night after church, a surgeon named Dr. Bob Schindler invited me to his house for a chat. I was honored that he would take time to do that. He shared with me the truth we've just presented to you, that we cannot trust our own judgment. He encouraged me to memorize Proverbs 3:5-6, where wise King Solomon wrote, "Trust in the LORD with all your heart; do not depend on your own understanding. Seek his will in all you do, and he will show you which path to take" (NLT).

I went home and memorized those verses and thought about them over and over before falling asleep. That night I had the two dreams that changed my life. Left to my own judgment, I might have become a carpenter instead of following God's true calling for me. But listening to a wise counselor made a huge difference in my life.

Dr. Schindler became a medical missionary to Africa and then served as the president of the Christian Medical and Dental Society. He went to be with the Lord a few years ago.

Honesty with Ourselves

Later in this book we'll discuss the importance of honesty in dealing with others. Just as important is self-honesty, which is often harder to recognize. What is self-honesty? Scripture describes it this way: "Never pay back evil with more evil. Do things in such a way that everyone can see you are honorable" (Romans 12:17, NLT).

An example of someone who has a problem with self-honesty involves a client we'll call Kevin. He is a teenager who was fired from his job at Wal-Mart for shoplifting. Sadly, this unfortunate incident has affected other areas of his life as well, because he lives in a small town where everybody is related to or knows everyone else. Since everyone in town knows about the incident, he has had a difficult time finding another job. The basketball coach refused to let Kevin play on the team after he heard about the incident, explaining that he did not want the other players to have to worry whether their belongings would be safe in the locker room. Kevin also has a criminal record now, which will most likely hurt his chances of being accepted into college.

Kevin's parents asked the Wal-Mart manager if he would consider dropping the charges and working out some other form of punishment, one that would not jeopardize the boy's future. But the manager refused, saying that at one time he was more than willing to drop the charges. In fact, he said Kevin was the first employee they had ever prosecuted, but Kevin had flatly refused to apologize or even acknowledge he had done anything wrong.

In counseling, Kevin stated that he thought stealing was indeed wrong, yet in his case it was permissible. He had ripped his pants while working at Wal-Mart a few weeks earlier. He had spoken with his supervisor, who had refused to pay for the pants, supposedly because the pants already had holes in them, put there by Kevin. Kevin had then decided that taking fifty dollars' worth of video games would square up everything. But one of the security guards witnessed him placing the games in his backpack and took the teenager into custody as he walked out of the store.

Kevin maintained his innocence throughout all the weeks of his counseling. Little could be done to help Kevin or his worried parents, because a person must acknowledge something before he or she can change it.

Most cases are not as blatant as Kevin's, but we do have to be careful, because our first instinct when someone wrongs us is to justify our desire to pay that person back. Your mind might say, *I owe him one!* but Scripture says to repay evil with good. Repaying evil with good is not natural and is difficult to do, especially at first. It goes against our natural feelings. But we don't (or shouldn't) live by our feelings in other areas of life, like work or school. If you skipped work every time you felt tired or did not feel like being there, what would happen?

In order to be honest with ourselves, we have to put aside emotion and look at our actions and attitudes through clear eyes.

Consider what the apostle Paul has to say on the subject of honesty:

> **We must live decent lives for all to see. Don't participate in the darkness of wild parties and drunkenness, or in sexual promiscuity and immoral living, or in quarreling and jealousy.**
> ROMANS 13:13, NLT

It's so easy to justify these types of behaviors in our lives. We see people in our offices every day who are caught up in these kinds of things, people who have convinced themselves they are not doing anything wrong. They are able to justify any behavior they please, even adultery and living with a partner before marriage. We hear excuses ranging from "We have to live together so we will really know if we're right for each other" to "It's no different than test driving a car before buying it." Yet numerous relationship studies clearly show that people who live together before marriage report a higher divorce rate and less-happy marriages.

How many times do we find ourselves in strife with someone else yet justifying our actions because we think the situation is the other person's fault? How many times do we allow jealousy to distort our thinking? It is very easy to live wrongly and justify it by convincing ourselves that we are doing everything right. Eventually, however, this mind-set robs our lives of joy, blessing, and peace. The best way to guard against this loss is by practicing self-honesty, which will grow as we set apart time to study God's Word and ask God to help us evaluate our lives and enable us to achieve lives characterized by honesty in every aspect.

Honesty with Others

We have examined the importance of honesty before God and with ourselves. Now let's look at the importance of honesty with others. If you were to ask people who know you to rank your honesty on a scale from 1 to 10, what would they say? Can others count on you as someone who is trustworthy? Honesty with others is of paramount importance.

Dishonesty is very hard to justify, even though it is so rampant in our world. In fact, think about how many barriers our society has put in place to force honesty. Video cameras are everywhere—in stores, schools, and gas stations. If you want to write a check, you have to show your driver's license to prove your identity, and then the check has to clear a verification process. If you want to borrow money from a bank, you'll find that they'll be happy to give you a loan only after you have proven you don't need one. Even contracts are set up on the presupposition that one or more parties will not be honest.

In the 1950s, farmers often earned extra money by setting up stands next to the highway. No one tended the stands; the farmers would just set out a few bushels of apples, pears, or other produce and leave signs with the prices. At the end of the day, the farmers picked up the remaining unsold fruit and the baskets of money people had left to pay for what they had taken. People could be trusted.

If you did that today, more than likely the fruit and the money would be gone within an hour, and the stand itself would probably be gone as well. Many in our society truly believe that if they can outsmart the system, they deserve whatever benefits they receive from doing that. We all hear people make statements such as, "That cashier gave me back too much change, but I shouldn't have to give it back to make up for her mistake."

One of the most dishonest ways we deal with others is through passive-aggressive behavior. Passive-aggressiveness is acting like a friend to a person's face but acting hurtfully behind that person's back. Someone involved in this sort of behavior hopes to frustrate another person without having to take responsibility for his or her own actions. This behavior is often seen in married and dating couples when one partner is angry with the other. The primary emotion behind passive-aggressive behavior is resentment.

We know a man who hated his cruel father. The father insisted that the son get a master's degree in business administration. The son actually loved business, so he did go to college and then graduate school to get his MBA. He took every MBA course and turned in every assignment—except for his final one, a simple five-page paper he could have written in an hour. He knew getting an MBA would please the father he resented, so he never turned in the last paper.

We know another man whose wife gave him a weekly list of honey-do chores. He resented her for being such a perfectionist, and he resented her for bossing him around as if he were her son. But he was afraid of her rejection and afraid to share his feelings with her, so when she asked him to mow the grass, he left streaks in the lawn. When she asked him to hang Christmas lights, he used giant nails to hang cheap lights on their expensive home. When the wife asked him to paint the inside of the house, he painted all the windows shut. Then whenever he wanted to make love at night, she developed a headache to return the favor.

If you are a teenager with a domineering parent, you may become passive-aggressive without even realizing it. You might even unconsciously express your anger toward your parents by displacing that anger on other authority figures and turning in papers late, skipping classes, or being late for appointments.

Passive-aggressiveness is so named because it uses passive means to aggressively hurt someone. This behavior undercuts and attempts to sabotage another person (or to sabotage yourself if you hold grudges against yourself for past failures), even as you deny you are doing it, or say you are doing the exact opposite. Passive-aggressiveness is also an attempt to hurt someone else while you manipulate circumstances to your benefit and justify your own wrong actions.

▶ *Todd Clements*

Sadly, the clearest example I can think of concerning passive-aggressive behavior involves myself. I spent two years of my college career in a fraternity house, an experience I wouldn't trade for a million dollars—or repeat for ten million. That style of community living brings out the "mooch" in some people. One guy in our fraternity had the notion that others' belongings were free game for him to borrow—with or without their knowledge. One day, on a trip to the lake, he helped himself to the only baseball cap I owned, not bothering to ask permission.

Several days later I realized the cap was missing and asked around to see if anyone might have it. More than one person informed me that this guy had been wearing it on the lake trip the past weekend. I asked him about it, and he told me yes, he had borrowed it, but at the end of the day he had given it to another guy who was supposed to bring it back to me.

The other guy swore he had never been given the cap, and I believed him. I then went back to the first guy and told him the other guy never had it. His reply to this was, "He's lying to you." Pretty frustrated and not wanting to make a scene, I dropped the argument (this was back in the days before I told it like it was).

The following Sunday morning I decided to go jogging before church. Walking through our parking lot I spotted the brand-new red 300Z sports car belonging to the guy who lost my hat. The closer I got to that car, the more I thought about the hat ordeal from a few days before. The more I thought about the ordeal, the angrier I became. As I walked by his car, I took the key to my room (already in my hand), reached out, and scraped his car on the passenger side from the back to the front.

I never looked back to assess the damage, but I knew it was substantial because I could hear metal scratching metal. As I continued, the thought crossed my mind, That'll show him for messing with my baseball cap.

That evening in our weekly members' meeting, everyone was ranting and raving that the fraternity next door had been vandalizing our vehicles. I simply nodded in agreement.

Another form of passive-aggressive behavior is purposely not doing things you say you will do. The wife of a couple we counseled admitted that she had been throwing away some of her husband's mail. She volunteered each day to drive to the post office to pick it up, so she had control of what happened to the mail. Eventually her passive-aggressive behavior caught up with her, as so often happens. She had continually discarded items from the IRS that were addressed to her husband, and after more than a year of no response, the IRS placed both the man and his wife under investigation. She was found guilty of tax fraud along with her husband, because he had been filing their taxes jointly. In order to avoid jail she had to work a second job to help pay the fines they owed. Her actions suddenly didn't seem so funny.

Passive-aggressive behavior ruins relationships, and it will also ruin your reputation if your behaviors are brought to the light. One day God will bring all our behaviors to the light and judge them. We read in 1 Corinthians 4:5:

> **Therefore judge nothing before the appointed time; wait till the Lord comes. He will bring to light what is hidden in darkness and will expose the motives of men's hearts. At that time each will receive his praise from God.**

If you are involved in this sort of behavior, be honest with yourself and work to stop it. Passive-aggressive behavior, if unchecked, can become a way of life. It hurts others, it hurts you, and God sees it as plain as day. Examine your heart. What are your motives?

> **We are careful to be honorable before the Lord, but we also want everyone else to see that we are honorable.**
>
> 2 CORINTHIANS 8:21, NLT

The Bottom Line

In this chapter, we saw how easy it is to be deceptive, especially when we feel justified in our response. But look again at the passage from Romans 12:

> **Do all that you can to live in peace with everyone. Dear friends, never take revenge. Leave that to the righteous anger of God. For the Scriptures say, "I will take revenge; I will pay them back," says the LORD. Instead, "If your enemies are hungry, feed them. If they are thirsty, give them something to drink. In doing this,**

> you will heap burning coals of shame on their heads." Don't let
> evil conquer you, but conquer evil by doing good.
>
> ROMANS 12:18-21, NLT

This biblical advice may seem crazy at first glance. In fact, this counsel goes against what popular culture says. But doing good to our enemies is exactly what the Bible teaches. Our main problem in obeying God here is lack of patience, especially when we've convinced ourselves that we are right.

That problem would not exist if people received immediate payback for their behavior. But God chooses not to operate this way, and instead of waiting on God we want to take matters into our own hands. We want to play God, just as Satan himself did.

But God sees everything that happens on earth exactly as it is, and he promises to deal with it appropriately:

> For a day of anger is coming, when God's righteous judgment
> will be revealed. He will judge everyone according to what they
> have done.   ROMANS 2:5-6, NLT

Since God knows everything we think, say, and do, doesn't it just make sense that honesty is the best policy?

In the next chapter, we'll look at more lessons we've learned about lying since we knew it all.

CHAPTER 4

Lies Will Catch Up with You

So Always Tell the Truth

[Lying]—Man's most universal weakness.

QUOTED IN *MARK TWAIN AND I*, BY OPIE READ

✦

The most outrageous lies that can be invented will find believers if a man tells them with all his might.

MARK TWAIN IN A LETTER TO *ALTA CALIFORNIA*, MAY 17, 1867

THE FIRST TWO PSYCHIATRIC diagnoses ever made were *idiot* and *imbecile*. That's right. People with mental problems in the 1800s were classified into one of these two groups. In fact, numerous papers were written to help physicians distinguish between an idiot and an imbecile.

Surprisingly, we still see clients who suffer from these two conditions today. These are people who tell lies rather than the truth. Read the following story and see if you can determine which category I (Dr. Clements) fall into—idiot or imbecile.

▶ *Todd Clements*

When I was in college, I tried to pull off what every guy dreams of: having two girlfriends at the same time. The whole arrangement just sort of happened, and I had the stupidity to go along with it. This feat took some work, as this occurred back in the dark ages before caller ID and cell phones. We had to answer the phone without knowing who was on the other end! How did we make it back then?

I didn't set out to have two girlfriends. It wasn't one of those, Hey, I've got two girlfriends. Man, isn't that cool? *deals. In fact, I knew I couldn't even brag about it, because as soon as I did, my secret would be out and I'd be in trouble. Only my two roommates knew, and they agreed not to spill the beans. But they couldn't agree with what was wrong with me—one said I was an imbecile, and the other called me an idiot.*

When I had first come to college, I still had a girlfriend at home. She was younger and still in high school, so we saw each other on the weekends. During the fall semester, however, I met a girl at college and we became friends. As the semester progressed we grew closer, and soon I had feelings for her. I began skipping trips home on the weekend so I could attend college events with this girl. She grew up in a small town on the other side of the state, and she had never even heard of my hometown or known anyone from there. This was great for me, or so I thought.

My feelings for my college girlfriend continued to grow, and I found myself wanting to spend more time with her. I finally made up my mind that it was time to break up with my hometown girlfriend. She was a great girl, and I knew it would be difficult to break the news to her. But as I prepared my speech ahead of time, I knew it had to be done. I planned to travel home the very next weekend and end it.

The next day, my college girlfriend delivered some surprising news that changed all my plans. She had been accepted to study in England for the spring semester. She would be gone for three months—January, February, and March. Wow!

I smiled excitedly on the outside as she told me the news, but on the inside my thoughts were racing. I felt like one of those swans you see gently circling in a pond. They glide gracefully and smoothly across the water with such a calm demeanor. Although it looks so effortless, under the water their legs are churning back and forth at warp speed. On the outside I was calm, but on the inside I was already scheming.

I'm sure you've already guessed what my pickled little brain was thinking. Why break up with hometown girl and be all alone while college girl was in England? I only had to juggle both of them until Christmas, which seemed easy enough. Christmas was only two months away. I figured I could hang with hometown girl over the winter and break up with her right before college girl came home. Perfect!

My roommates laughed in my face when I told them the solution to my female predicament. One remarked that I was about to find out how small the world really is. They even made bets with each other on which girl would find out first and how soon it would happen.

The plan went according to schedule the first month with no problems. I told my college girlfriend that I needed to go home every other weekend to help my father on the farm. While at home, I explained to my girlfriend there that the large amount of coursework would probably keep me in the library every other weekend.

*Christmas would be the last big hurdle. I started early to pre-
pare my college girl for the news that I would need to go home
over Christmas break to work. I told my hometown girl that
I might need to travel across the state to visit a college friend
during the break. She naturally assumed it was a guy friend.
When the holidays arrived, an ice storm blanketed the area
and restricted any travel. I was disappointed that I would have
to say good-bye to the college girl over the phone. I knew I
would miss her tremendously over the next three months, but
I breathed a sigh of relief as we hung up the phone. It was
over; I had pulled it off and now had no more worries.*

*College girl arrived in England and started school, faithfully
writing me every Sunday. Hometown girl and I saw each other
on weekends here in the United States. When our college's
rugby team asked me to kick for them that upcoming spring,
I accepted and began to practice each day. In February our
team traveled to play an exhibition game against another university. Hometown girl had a good friend who attended the
school we were playing, so she drove up to watch us play.
I looked forward to this fun weekend playing with the team
and spending time with hometown girl's friends.*

*Game time on Saturday afternoon rolled around, and I fig-
ured hometown girl and her friend must be running late
since they were not yet in the stands. Midway through the
first half, they still had not arrived. During the second half I
finally spotted hometown girl in the bleachers. Surprisingly,
she sat there alone. I waved when I saw her, and to this
day I will never forget her response. She glared a hole right
through me. I thought maybe she was just mad at her friend,
but when I approached hometown girl after the game, she*

maintained her ferocious glare and snarled, "You and I need to talk!"

"Okay, about what?" I asked.

"I don't think you want to find out right here in front of your friends," she answered.

"Sure I do," I said, ignorant of what was about to transpire.

I quickly learned that hometown girl had made it to her friend's sorority house that morning. She met her friend's roommate, who was from a small town in Arkansas—the same small town that college girlfriend came from. To make matters worse, college girlfriend happened to be one of this girl's best friends.

The roommate remembered college girlfriend saying that I was on the rugby team and that she ought to meet me when we came to town. She asked hometown girl if she could come with her and meet this guy whose name she could not remember.

Then the roommate started looking through her letters from college girlfriend to find out my name. You can imagine hometown girl's surprise when she blurted, "Here it is. Todd Clements. Yeah, that's him." I don't know all that happened in the next hour, but somehow the two girls managed to phone college girlfriend, who verified everything. I was totally toast!

When hometown girl finished telling me what a sorry excuse for a human being I was, she relayed a message from college girlfriend. I can't repeat it here because I want this book to be sold in family stores. Needless to say, both girls were finished with me. To make matters worse, the roommate had *already fixed up hometown girl with a date from her boy-friend's fraternity for that evening. The four of them were all going to a big party, which I wasn't invited to.*

The next Sunday, I sure got an interesting letter from college ex-girlfriend. My roommates were upset when I told them the story. Not because I got dumped by both girls but because they were not there to witness my downfall firsthand. They were right though; I did find out how small the world actually is.

I must have been an imbecile. Yes, lying hurts others, but in the end it hurts you the most. Nothing can trash your reputa-tion like lying. Once you are labeled a liar in someone's eyes, it's very hard to ever change that view.

What God Says about Lying

Let's look and see what the God who made the universe says about this subject:

> **You shall not give false testimony against your neighbor.**
> EXODUS 20:16

Giving false testimony means lying in court. If you take the stand as a witness in court, you put your hand on the Bible and repeat, "I swear to tell the truth, the whole truth, and nothing but the truth." This covers everything from telling half-truths, leaving out information, twisting the facts, and even inventing a falsehood. God expects us to be truthful not only in public but in private as well.

See what else God says about lying:

> **There are six things the LORD hates, seven that are detestable to him: haughty eyes, a lying tongue, hands that shed innocent blood, a heart that devises wicked schemes, feet that are quick**

> **to rush into evil, a false witness who pours out lies and a man**
> **who stirs up dissension among brothers.**   PROVERBS 6:16-19

Sexual sins are not even listed here, but lying is so important, it makes the list twice: once as a "lying tongue"—someone who is lying *to* someone else—and a second time as a "false witness"—someone who is lying *about* someone (or exaggerating or gossiping).

God views lying in the same way he views murder and pride. The fact that God hates lying ought to be reason enough not to lie. God hates sin because he loves people. And he hates lies because lies hurt people.

God loved college girl, hometown girl, and even me (Dr. Clements), in spite of my sins. He didn't want any of us to get hurt, but he also warned us that eventually our sins would be discovered. He may very well have arranged for this sequence of events to happen to help me become more like him.

If God had waited, I might have gotten away with it when I finally broke up with my hometown girlfriend in the spring. But I might also have been tempted to continue lying. After this humiliation and the severe guilt I felt about hurting two wonderful girls, both of whom I really did care about, I stopped my lying.

What exactly is lying? If a child asks you if the picture he drew is pretty, and it isn't, what do you say then? What about when Aunt Hilda asks you what you think of her new hairdo?

The Bible tells us to speak the truth in love, but doing so is a learned skill. You can tell Aunt Hilda, "That purple hair sticking straight out makes you look like a scary Martian." Or you can speak the truth in love by saying, "Well, I must say I have never seen another hairdo quite like it. It is really unique. How did you get the idea to fix it that way?" Both are truthful, but the latter is also respectful.

Quite often, people who routinely tell false tales think others do not realize they are lying. The reality, however, is that others usually do know the person is lying; they simply choose not to call him or her on it.

People Lie to Impress

Lying to impress others might seem harmless. We have worked with some patients who would never steal or try to hurt someone but would lie by saying what they think someone else wants to hear. This type of person is so afraid of rejection that lying has become a way of life. In the end, however, this action hurts the person who is lying and the people being lied to.

Often when we try to impress someone, we just end up looking silly. Once people realize we aren't truthful, everything else we say becomes suspect. The desire to impress others can tempt us to make false statements by bragging and exaggerating. But few people care to hang around someone who's bent on impressing others. The person who does this is caught up in herself, and no one wants to hang out with someone who talks about herself all the time.

A narcissist is an extreme example of this behavior. Narcissists love attention, but they are blind to their own narcissism. They believe they are more spiritual or better looking than they really are. Sometimes they sit in the front row at church and raise their hands at every song, supposedly to bring honor to God, but really (at least subconsciously) to show everyone how super spiritual they are. And at prayer meetings, they nearly always pray the longest prayers and in the most dramatic fashion.

Narcissists like to name-drop, acting as if they know important people better than they really do. We can usually diagnose a narcissist at the first appointment when that person calls us Paul or Todd, rather than Dr. Meier or Dr. Clements. These kinds of people always want special favors and expect to be seen without an appointment or get a prescription for a family member who is not one of our patients. When we deny one of their requests, they become hurt and angry.

When dealing with a narcissist, we've found that we need to be polite, but we also need to maintain a professional, rather than personal, relationship with these people.

Watch out for anyone who tells lies and flatters—they are out to get you. PROVERBS 26:28, CEV

This verse wonderfully ties flattery and lying together. Not only does the Bible warn of the foolishness of those who are taken in by flattery, it also warns of the sin of the flatterer.

> **They like themselves too much to hate their own sins or even to see them. They tell deceitful lies, and they don't have the sense to live right.** PSALM 36:2-3, CEV

> **May the LORD cut off all flattering lips and every boastful tongue.** PSALM 12:3

We see a lot of narcissistic characters on TV sitcoms, but in reality narcissism is no laughing matter, especially to God. Even though the person may mean no harm at all, the attitude is prideful and it deceives and hurts others.

People Lie When They Gossip

Gossip ruins intimate relationships, and we believe it wrecks more marriages and friendships than any other factor. Often, gossip is not completely true—which means it is a lie, and those who spread it are liars. However, when confronted, gossipers nearly always shirk responsibility, claiming they were only repeating what someone else was already saying. Even if the gossip turns out to be completely true (which it rarely is), it damages other people and tarnishes reputations.

Most Christians will agree that gossiping and telling white lies are sins, but somehow they have been classified as "minor" sins. In reality, there is no such thing as a minor sin in God's eyes. The Bible gives us warning after warning to avoid gossiping. The wisdom book of Proverbs mentions it four times:

> It's stupid to say bad things about your neighbors. If you are sensible, you will keep quiet. A gossip tells everything, but a true friend will keep a secret. —PROVERBS 11:12-13, CEV

> Gossip is no good! It causes hard feelings and comes between
> friends. —PROVERBS 16:28, CEV
> The words of a talebearer are as wounds, and they go down into
> the innermost parts of the belly. —PROVERBS 18:8, KJV
>> (The "belly" is symbolic here for the center of emotions. It is
>> used much like we use the word *heart* today.)
> Where there is no fuel a fire goes out; where there is no gossip
> arguments come to an end. —PROVERBS 26:20, CEV

Holy gossip is as great a sin as regular gossip. Holy gossip is asking
your Sunday school class to pray for Bob and Katie because they're
having marriage problems due to Bob's excessive drunkenness. Unless
you were asked by the couple to reveal their problem to the Sunday
school class, you've just tried to glorify gossip by disguising it as a prayer
request.

A word to the wise—some people will repeat whatever you tell them.
Often these people are kind, generous, and active in the church. They
may ask about your personal life pretending to be concerned for your
well-being, and then they'll usually deny the fact that they've repeated
your story to someone else. Don't waste your time trying to change them.
Learn discernment instead. You can still be a friend, but don't discuss
anything with them that you wouldn't want discussed word for word
with others.

You can identify these people because they are usually telling you
personal information about other people. Remember, if they tell you other
people's business, they're probably also telling other people your business.
Be careful about what you allow them to tell you. When they begin to share
someone's personal matters, just say, "I don't feel comfortable talking about
Emily when she's not here."

Yes, gossip is interesting, it gives people something to talk about
besides the weather, and it can seem harmless; but it also ruins friendships, splits churches, and stirs up strife. When people spend all of their

time talking about the problems of someone else, there is little time left to carry out God's work.

People Lie to Get Their Own Way

This third type of lying is the worst. These people lie not to impress or gossip but to get their way, and they don't care who they hurt in the process. These are people who would steal from you if they knew they wouldn't get caught.

One summer I (Dr. Clements) worked as a lifeguard for a country club. As the crowds waned near the end of the summer, the pool manager decided he needed to let one lifeguard go. I later discovered one of the other lifeguards told him several parents had complained that I spent most of my time talking rather than watching the pool. This was totally false. Thankfully, the boss didn't take his word but instead watched us from inside the country club with binoculars. When he realized the lifeguard accusing me was actually the one who visited with the girls, the boss fired the guy who had bad-mouthed me. This situation worked out, but many times it doesn't, and the liar prevails.

The Bible strongly warns against this type of liar:

> Truth will last forever; lies are soon found out.
> —PROVERBS 12:19, CEV
> The LORD hates every liar, but he is the friend of all who can be trusted. Be sensible and don't tell everything you know—only fools spread foolishness everywhere.   —PROVERBS 12:22-23, CEV
> Telling lies about friends is like attacking them with clubs and swords and sharp arrows.   —PROVERBS 25:18, CEV

The Bottom Line

Our society often downplays the act of lying. Some cultures even embrace it. But the person who routinely lies will find heartache. He or she will have little respect, few friends, and no sympathy from God. Every one of us is prone to lie. Sometimes we do it so regularly that we don't even realize what we are doing.

Lying creates harmful tensions, because the liar has a difficult time remembering whom he or she told what to. Life is much easier and your self-worth so much better when you become a person of honesty and integrity.

I (Dr. Meier) accidentally drove through a tollbooth a few weeks ago without paying the toll, but not because I was trying to cheat the authorities out of a few cents. I had my mind on work and completely missed the stop. So when I got to the next tollbooth, I paid double.

"Why are you paying double?" the tollbooth attendant asked.

"Because it's worth a lot more than forty cents to have a feeling of integrity and honesty," I replied.

Think about all the people in government and business and even in our churches who go through life lying and hurting people just to get a little more money. As psychiatrists, we know that the only truly happy people in this world are those who deeply love and are deeply loved by God, others, and themselves (in a biblical way). At the end of your life, what lifestyle will you wish you had chosen? Why not choose it right now?

CHAPTER 5

Dating Often Leads to Marriage

So Only Date Someone You'd Be Willing to Marry

Love is not a product of reasoning and statistics. It just comes—none knows whence—and cannot explain itself.

MARK TWAIN, *EVE'S DIARY*

I (DR. MEIER) HAD A GOOD FRIEND who dated a girl in our high school, though he claimed he didn't really like her even after a year and a half together.

"Why don't you break up with her?" I'd sometimes ask him.

"Well, she's got a nice family that likes me, and I don't want to hurt her feelings or embarrass her," he'd explain.

"Then what are you going to do?"

"I'll go to a college several hours away. Since she's two years younger than I am and has to stay here to finish high school, our relationship can just die out," he answered.

Sadly, my friend's plan didn't work out the way he expected. He did go to another state for college, but he underestimated this girl's resolve. She drove up to his college every Friday afternoon and stayed until Sunday night.

A few years later, as we were putting on our tuxes for his wedding, I asked if he was sure he wanted to get married.

"Why are you asking me that?" he asked.

"Because of the conversations we've had in the past," I reminded him.

"Well, I guess she finally grew on me," he replied.

I really hoped that this was the case, but years later my friend confided that he was chronically unhappy and hated his life. He said, "Almost every night when I go to bed, I dread the next morning. The next morning I dread the upcoming day. I wish I had my life to do over, but I don't. I'm also stuck now because I have kids and responsibilities."

I had just started practicing psychiatry, so you'd expect me to have a wonderful answer for him. But I could not think of one helpful thing to say. Oh, I knew what I wanted to say: "We all tried to warn you in high school and college, but you refused to listen, so you're getting what you deserve!" But what good would that do except to heap more coals on his head? That's when I decided the best way to help someone with this problem was by preventing it, by teaching people how to avoid making such a mistake in the first place.

Who was to blame in this story? Do you think the girl might have been at fault? In reality she was sweet and beautiful, and she had a wonderful personality. Why did her husband have such a hard time loving her? I don't know. I even had a different friend who was in love with this young woman for years and who always hoped she would break up with the other guy.

Do we feel sorry for the man in this situation? A little. Do we feel sorry for the woman? Most definitely! A guy she loved for years led her on, telling her he loved her. She got stuck with a man who was depressed and no fun to be around, and she received little emotional support.

What if the friend had bitten the bullet in high school and confessed that his girlfriend was just not the person for him? Sure it would have hurt her, and her family would have been upset too. But they would have gotten over it, and she would most likely have fallen in love again.

What might have happened if the other man—the one who was enthralled by her—had been given the chance to date her? We can never know if she would have fallen in love with him, but she might have. What about the man who married her? He probably could have found someone else and fallen in love. But now it was too late. The dream had turned into a nightmare.

Why Do We Fall for the Wrong People?

When two young people fall in love, they both dream of everlasting, unconditional love. They spend hours talking about their dreams for the future and envisioning what it will be like to grow old together surrounded by children and grandchildren. Although in the early stages of love a couple's dreams rarely include the inevitable times of difficulty, sadness, or discouragement, even these trials can help to build and strengthen lifelong love.

But with the wrong person, optimistic dreams can quickly turn into a nightmare. There are many reasons you might find yourself with the wrong person:

1. To fill the love vacuum left by a parent.
2. To try to "fix" a parent's faults by "fixing" a partner whose traits are similar to that parent.
3. To get revenge on a neglectful or abusive parent by getting vengeance on a partner.
4. To live up to the predictions of parents who said you didn't deserve better or weren't smart enough to make decisions for yourself.

Many Americans today wish they were not married to their current spouse. How does this happen? It all begins with the dating relationship.

They date the wrong person

As professionals who counsel adolescents and young adults, we hear this frequently: "We're just dating. There's no way I would marry a guy/girl like that." We're sorry to be the bearers of bad news, but this attitude is sad, selfish, and harmful for both of you. When you make a statement like this, you're saying that the person you're dating does not meet your standards. Believe it or not, many people who make such statements actually end up together, usually because someone's standards have been lowered.

We sometimes hear this reason given for choosing a spouse: "But he (or she) is a good Christian man (or woman)." That's great, but just because somebody is a Christian does not mean you are supposed to marry him or her. Don't let family or friends use that reasoning to try to persuade you to date or marry someone.

They're filling a void

Another reason a young person might choose to date the wrong mate has to do with a psychological principle called transference reaction. This is based on what our parents are like, how they interacted with each other, and other aspects of their marriage that formed our opinions about the way men and women relate, opinions which are often set in place by the age of six.

What the world calls falling in love is no more than a transference reaction of your emotions from your parent of the opposite sex to a substitute your own age. Eighty-five percent of people choose a mate who is very similar to his or her parent of the opposite sex. If you are a young woman whose dad was an abusive alcoholic, you might have a tendency to "fall in love" with abusive alcoholics.

If you are a young man who had a domineering mother, you will have crushes on domineering women. Sometimes this reverses and you fall in love with whichever parent-type you felt most neglected by, so a man may fall in love with a woman whose personality is like his dad's and vice versa.

If you have a loving mother and a loving father who treat you with dignity, you are very fortunate. If you have been treated with dignity all your life, you will not put up with being in a relationship with the wrong person due to transference reaction. But if your parents treated you badly and were highly critical, you'll tend to believe those lies and look for a mate who will reinforce whatever bad treatment you are used to. We are all born with a father vacuum, a mother vacuum, and a God vacuum. The more unloved we felt by a particular parent growing up, the more we crave someone to fill the father or mother vacuum in our lives.

This transference reaction feels really good, releasing endorphins and other chemicals into our brains. That is why these kinds of relationships feel so right in the beginning. A puppy-love crush can last anywhere from eighteen minutes to eighteen months, but it seldom lasts forever. Therefore, it is a good idea to date a person seriously for longer than eighteen months before you agree to get married.

They're too needy

The needier you are, the more you will miss any bad behaviors in the person you are dating. Often, a woman who is needy will reluctantly give in and have sex with her partner because she believes that this father substitute really loves her. Young and naive, the woman is then surprised when she is dumped for someone else—a "new body."

▶ *Paul Meier*

As a young girl, Mary was sexually and physically abused by her alcoholic father. Her mother was passive and nonprotective. Because her father vacuum was never filled with real love, Mary craved male attention. Unfortunately, she always seemed to fall for alcoholics or drug addicts who sexually and physically abused her. Even though she became a Christian in college, she never dated any kind, loving Christian men because she found them "too boring."

Mary ultimately became a famous movie star. Though she had wealth, good looks, and charisma, she had married and divorced eight different men by the time she was thirty-six.

After her eighth divorce, Mary came to me for counseling. I asked how such an intelligent, attractive, and wealthy young woman could make the same mistake eight straight times. She blamed it on bad luck, explaining that all eight of her husbands had seemed to be nice guys when she married them. I showed her that she had been unknowingly choosing husbands who were just like her dad. She got so angry with me that she left the session. But she came back in a few days, realizing I was right. She was ready to make a change, she said, and was willing to do whatever it took. We worked together for three straight weeks, healing her wounds from the past and focusing on God's plan for her future. She did well from then on but decided never to marry again.

If an intelligent, talented woman like Mary could so easily make consistently poor choices in dating and marriage, can you see how easy it would be for any of us to do the same? Rather than trusting our own judgment, we must seek God's wisdom to develop the right approach to dating and marriage.

> **Trust in the LORD with all your heart and lean not on your own understanding; in all your ways acknowledge him, and he will make your paths straight.** PROVERBS 3:5-6

How Can We Be Sure We're Dating the Right People?

So what does the Bible say about dating and marriage? Nothing, actually. We have no evidence that people in biblical times really dated; marriages were most likely arranged by families. It sounds strange to us, but that was their culture. (They would find our culture just as strange, we're sure.)

But the Bible does talk a lot about relationships in general. In 2 Corinthians 6:14, the apostle Paul warns us: "Do not be yoked together with unbelievers." A yoke is a harness that connects two oxen or cattle and allows them to pull farm equipment, such as heavy plows or grinding wheels. In a similar way, marriage yokes two people together to pull in the same direction.

Paul states it quite clearly: If you are a Christian, don't marry a non-Christian. That certainly does eliminate a large portion of the playing field, doesn't it? God is not trying to take away your fun. He simply wants to save you and your family from heartache. Trust us on this, please, and don't go looking for loopholes. Missionary dating—when a Christian dates a non-Christian hoping to convert him or her—rarely works.

As psychologists, we often hear this question: "What if I am going out with someone I really love, but I don't know for sure if he is a Christian?" Fortunately, God has given most of us common sense. It won't take long for a person's actions to reveal what he or she believes and values.

When it comes to relationships, most of what the Bible deals with occurs after marriage. In Matthew 19 Jesus told the Pharisees that God intended marriage to be permanent:

> **Moses permitted you to divorce your wives because your hearts were hard. But it was not this way from the beginning. I tell you that anyone who divorces his wife, except for marital unfaithfulness, and marries another woman commits adultery.**
>
> MATTHEW 19:8-9

This brings up the question, "How do I know if the person I'm dating is the right person?" The answer depends on common sense, logic, and prayer.

Use common sense

Be honest with yourself as you answer the following questions.

> How do I feel about this person?
> How does this person feel about me?
> Am I in love with this person?

> Do I *like* this person? Remember that like is different from love. We can love people as God would love them, but that doesn't necessarily mean that we like them (or that they like us).

  For example, Dave was engaged to Joyce years ago. Joyce's father asked Dave what he thought of Joyce.

  Dave said, "I love her."

  Her father then asked, "But do you like her?"

  Dave realized he didn't, and he called off the marriage before he made a costly mistake.

> Does this person put me first?
> Can I picture myself being with this person for the rest of my life?
> Does my family like this person?
> Do my friends like this person?
> Do I like this person's family?
> Do I like this person's friends?
> Does this person treat me with respect?
> Is this person concerned with my happiness?
> Do I trust this person 100 percent?

  If you can't trust your partner, you'll spend enormous amounts of energy wondering where he is during the day and what he is doing. The thought *Could he be cheating on me?* will never leave.

Use logic

Ask yourself, *How well do we* fit *together?* Again be honest with yourself about the following questions:

> Do we both want to live in the same area?
> Do I approve of and support this person's career plans?
> Would I be satisfied living on this person's salary?
> Do we agree on the issue of having children?
> Do we agree on the best way to raise children?

> Do we agree on the husband's and wife's roles in marriage?

This question has become even more important in today's multiethnic society with intercultural marriages. Some cultures' views regarding traditional marriage roles differ widely from others'. Although the Bible says a man will leave his father and mother and cleave to his wife, many ethnic groups consider the husband's culture to be the dominant one in a marriage.

> Do we agree on church?

This subject can wreck your marriage if it is not dealt with. It can be touchy, especially if you are from different denominations. You might agree to attend your own separate churches (which we do not recommend, by the way), but if you do, you'll still need to decide what to do when children arrive.

Pray

God is the final authority. Only he knows the depth of your feelings toward your partner. Only he knows whose hearts actually belong to him. Only he knows what the future holds. Only he knows your mate better than you do.

God wants you to marry the person of your dreams. He wants you to live life to the fullest. But he also expects you to put him first, even above your mate. Putting your mate ahead of God is considered idolatry, a sin that God puts in the same category with witchcraft (Galatians 5:19-20).

God does not want to hide his will for you in this area, but if he knows you are resistant to following his will, he may remain silent on the issue. If you feel you have been praying with no answer, ask yourself if you've truly been willing to hear what God is saying to you. And if so, are you willing to respond based on what he reveals to you?

We often hear clients say, "Yeah I know I should break up with her, but I miss her when I do, so we get back together."

▶ *Paul Meier*

When I was younger, I'd break up with my girlfriend, then drive myself crazy wondering what she was up to. I'd call her, and we would get back together, and the cycle would start again. Finally my mother realized what was happening and showed me that I wasn't lonely because I missed her, but rather I missed her because I was lonely.

Times of aloneness are part of being single, but it is better to be single and alone than to be with someone and lonely. There is a difference between aloneness and loneliness.

God understands the sadness you feel when you are lonely. He loves you. He thinks about you so many times each day that you could not possibly count them (Psalm 139:17-18, NLT). Think about that.

Avoid the myth of the perfect mate

Many people believe that God prepares someone specifically for each person and then sees to it that each pairing ends up together. But if that were true, why do four out of five Christian adults wish they had married a different person?

On rare occasions God leads an Isaac to a Rebekah, but he uses different approaches to unite different people. He doesn't want us to be robots. He gives us choices to make about whether to marry, whom to marry, where to live, what career to pursue, what colleges to attend, what clothes to wear, what movies to see, which church will fit our particular needs and preferences, and so on.

As psychiatrists, we have spent many hours listening to women in their forties who are depressed and lonely because they believe the myth of the perfect mate and have been waiting for twenty or more years for the perfect men to knock on their doors.

We have also spent many hours listening to women who believed that they married the men God chose for them, only to find out they had been conned.

God's will is that we serve him and become like him. He really doesn't care whether or not we get married. But if we do, he wants us to marry committed Christians. There may be a million Christian men or women in this world that God would be equally pleased for you to marry.

God clearly defines his purpose for us in Romans 8:29:

> **For those God foreknew he also predestined to be conformed to the likeness of his Son, that he might be the firstborn among many brothers.**

More than anything else, God wants us to develop Christlikeness.

Another myth we hear all too often is this: "If God wants us to be together, then it will work out." That's as ridiculous as saying, "I'm going to cross this busy freeway at night with my eyes closed, wearing black pants and a black shirt. If God doesn't want me to get hit by a car, then I won't." Then what happens? Three steps and *wham!* Next thing you know, you're waking up in the intensive care unit and wondering why God wanted that car to hit you.

If you try to force God to make a decision by refusing to make a decision yourself, your refusal is actually a decision. Why? Because God gave us free will. If he forces a decision upon us, there is no free will.

People also like to use this same myth when they break up: "If God wants us to get back together, he'll work it out." But what the person is actually saying is this: "I want to break up with you, but I don't want you to be mad at me. So I blame us not being together on God. Then you can be mad at him rather than me. Also, if I can't find someone else, I can still come back to you, and you will have to take me back because it is God's will. At least that's what I want you to believe."

In psychiatry we call this spiritualizing—using God as an excuse to escape your responsibility. You are spiritualizing when you tell your boss, "I know I was thirty minutes late for work today, but God must not have wanted me to be here until now because he put an awful traffic jam in my way." (Did you expect him to part traffic for you or wake you up thirty minutes earlier?)

The Bottom Line

When it comes to dating and marriage, make your own decisions as God prompts you, and then take responsibility for those decisions. When you pray for an answer, be willing to accept that answer.

Here are some final dos and don'ts to keep in mind regarding dating and marriage.

> Don't be afraid or embarrassed to back out of a wedding.
> A Christian marriage is a lifelong commitment.
> Don't marry someone unless you can accept him or her just the way he or she is—faults and all. It is highly unlikely that you will be able to change your mate.
> Get to know a variety of different Christians of the opposite sex, so you will have a broader understanding of what kind of people you enjoy spending time with and what kind you don't. This will be especially helpful when you are deciding who you want to spend the rest of your life with.
> Attend some sessions with a trained Christian psychologist or licensed therapist who understands human dynamics and can warn you of potential pitfalls.
> When you find someone who treats you with dignity and for whom you still have romantic feelings after eighteen months, consider that person a potential mate. Seek premarital counseling and psychological testing.
> Don't have sex or even go beyond a hug and a kiss before you get married. If you refuse to let people use your body, the users will ditch you, and the good ones will hang around to fall in love with your soul.

CHAPTER 6

Marriage Is Hard Work

So Do Your Homework

When you fish for love, bait with your heart, not your brain.

MARK TWAIN, "NOTEBOOK," 1898

APPROXIMATELY 50 PERCENT OF marriages in the United States now end in divorce. And of those who stay together, many report unhappy marriages. Every unhappily married person we know is unhappy in other areas of life as well.

If so many of us dream of happy marriages, why are nearly 80 percent of Americans disappointed, divorced, or stuck in marriages they consider mistakes?[1] The reason is simple: People don't do their homework, either before the marriage or afterward.

In the last chapter, we talked about the range of problems that can occur when you date someone you wouldn't consider marrying. In this chapter, we'll briefly examine other pitfalls to a good marriage. While some people like to brag about learning lessons the hard way, marriage is not something anybody wants to learn about the hard way!

▶ *Todd Clements*

"Do you have any young, single doctor friends you could introduce me to, Dr. Clements?" asked Vanessa.

"Why? Are you having some kind of medical problem?" I replied, trying to hold back my laughter. It's not every day I get asked that question by a sixteen-year-old in our therapy group. Oblivious to my sarcasm, she replied, "No, I want to go out with him. I've wanted to marry a doctor since I was young."

Rather than blow off this young girl's naïveté, I decided to use the group to teach Vanessa a vital lesson. Peer groups are great because teenagers are often more willing to take advice and criticism from someone in their own age group than from me. I promptly put the ball in play by asking, "So, do you think you are doctor's wife material?" The group quickly jumped in and began to point out that this drug-abusing high school dropout would need a lot more maturity if she ever hoped to marry a doctor. Vanessa, however, defended her shortcomings with a statement I hear frequently: "Well, if we really fell in love, that stuff wouldn't matter to him."

Vanessa's mind-set includes two popular misconceptions that could be setting her up for future heartache. They are the "looking-for-Mr.-Right syndrome" and the "Romeo-and-Juliet syndrome."

Even if you marry the nicest guy in the world, the marriage won't work out if *you* aren't the right person. We spend so much time looking for Mr. or Ms. Right, but we rarely spend time becoming the right person ourselves.

We've often heard people say they have prayed that God would send them the right person to marry. Sometimes parents, grandparents, and the whole family have been praying too. Whenever we hear this, we'll ask them to describe the kind of person they want God to send them. Then we'll ask, "If this same person were praying for God to send him the right person to marry, would God send you?"

You can answer the question of who you should marry using a two-part equation: a person is only right for you if you are right for him or her.

Society embraces Romeo-and-Juliet love—the belief that nothing else matters but love. Add this kind of blind love to insurmountable odds and you have the perfect recipe for romance. Sadly, however, couples who buy into this way of thinking rarely make it in real life. Even Romeo and Juliet committed suicide in the end.

True love is the foundation of a great marriage, but it's not the whole house. What our culture refers to as "falling in love" is actually a puppy-love crush stemming from transference reactions. As we've already seen, these kinds of crushes last anywhere from eighteen minutes to eighteen months, and then they are gone. Unfortunately, many couples mistake these crushes for true love and marry during the eighteen-month period, only to discover later that they have "fallen out of love."

Do Opposites Attract or Attack?

Surprisingly, the factors that we usually focus on the most in a relationship—wealth, age, looks, education, and career—have less importance than we think when it comes to long-term happiness. These characteristics are not unimportant, but they should not be the core issues your relationship is based upon.

While shared interests can bring a couple together, common values are much more important. It's been said that interests make a relationship interesting, but values make a relationship valuable. It's critical that you understand the difference between values and interests. A lot of people still think a value refers to the blue light special at Kmart. But it's much more than that. While interests change like the wind, values are at the core of what we are. An interest in politics may lead you to become a politician, but your values will determine what kind of politician you are.

Whenever we counsel couples, we ask them to describe the values they admire in one another. Answers often include "He's a good cook" or "She always keeps the house clean." But these are not values, which take time to discern and involve some depth. Interests may be what first attracts us to someone, but values are what keep us attracted to that unique person.

God made each of us as one-of-a-kind individuals (even identical twins), with different interests and values. No two people are exactly the same. Different interests are often reconcilable, unless they are radically different. And sometimes, too many differences make it too difficult for a couple to create a lasting commitment.

▶ *Todd Clements*

One of my favorite things to do is spend time at my family's hunting lodge. It's in the beautiful Ozark Mountains, and the peaceful fresh air there creates a perfect escape from the city. Shortly after we were married, my wife admitted that spending weekends at the lodge bored her to tears. I couldn't believe it at first, but then I decided she just needed to learn to like hunting so she would enjoy coming to the lodge.

I badgered her until she finally agreed to go deer hunting with me. To this day, she still says those were the worst two hours of her life, and they were probably mine as well. She squirmed in her seat the whole time, coughed loudly, talked out loud, and shivered from the cold after only one hour. I foolishly persuaded her to stay out with me another hour after she complained that she couldn't feel her fingers anymore. She later admitted that she had talked out loud on purpose because she didn't want to see me kill a deer.

Later that year my wife started making scrapbooks in her leisure time. Luckily, she was wise enough not to try and make me scrapbook. Now we both look forward to weekends at the hunting lodge. She scrapbooks by the fireplace while I spend time out in the woods.

Interests can change and be modified. You might be interested in playing golf but find that in order to make a relationship work you need to compromise and not golf *every* weekend.

Values are more rigid. In *Call It Love or Call It Quits,* Tim Timmons and Charlie Hedges talk about two kinds of values: motivating values and driving values. Motivating values reflect your attitude toward money, status, security, and comfort. These values can be bent, although not easily. For instance, if you highly value money, you might want to work all the time to earn more of it. But in order to spend time with your partner, you might also need to compromise and not work so many hours.

Driving values, on the other hand, come from our understanding of right and wrong and our beliefs about God. These are convictions we will fight for and maybe even die for. Driving values concern justice, honesty, integrity, and spirituality. It is almost impossible to compromise our driving values. Our faith system is one of our most important driving values. To compromise what we believe about God in order to please our partners would be a terrible mistake. In the last chapter, we saw the wise warning the apostle Paul gives us against this:

> Do not be yoked together with unbelievers. For what do righteousness and wickedness have in common? Or what fellowship can light have with darkness?
>
> 2 CORINTHIANS 6:14

Compromising your relationship with God is a high price to pay for companionship. We have counseled many couples who faced this issue. Some say that everything was fine until children came along. Even if the children are freely allowed to choose which faith to follow, they are usually confused as to which to choose. The only couples we have seen who did not have trouble with this issue were those in which both partners had little interest in their spiritual lives. If you want to be truly happy in your marriage, find someone who shares the same values in life as you do.

Avoid the *Love Boat* Syndrome

The Love Boat was a popular television series in the 1980s. The sitcom/drama was set on a cruise ship, where people from all walks of life came together. During the cruise, passengers mixed and mingled and invariably paired off with other passengers or crew members. These new couples usually ended their trip with a romp in the bedroom during the last night or two of the cruise.

The last night of the cruise always presented the same question: What would happen now that the trip was over? Was it simply a weeklong fling, or had they met the loves of their lives? Some realized they had been used and got dumped, but other couples quickly got engaged or married.

We know it was just a silly TV show, but many people do this in real life, getting married before they have time to know the other person. Some people spend more time studying for a test than they do deciding which person to marry.

The first thing to do when making a decision about your future mate is to avoid the "*Love Boat* Syndrome." Take everything you've learned about marriage from television and movies and throw it away. James Bond is no more in love with a different woman every adventure than he could really kill dozens of people shooting at him without breaking a sweat or ever being grazed by a bullet. Hollywood's portrayal of marriage is one dimensional, based solely on physical attraction.

But wait a minute, you might say. What about all those people who claim to have experienced love at first sight when they first saw their future spouses? In reality, they're describing physical attraction at first sight that progressed into love later. People who buy into love at first sight obviously have an extremely shallow definition of love. How can somebody love you if they don't even know you? Physical attraction is important, but it is not love. If love were the foundation of a house, physical attraction would form the walls. And walls without a foundation blow over the first time a storm comes through. Yes, you can have love without physical attraction, but a house without walls is pretty hollow.

Not all couples who get married right off the bat end up unhappy. Many go on to have successful, lifelong marriages. However, statistics prove that the divorce rate is higher for those people who marry in haste.[2]

People often ask us how long they should date someone before getting married. And while there is no hard-and-fast rule, we usually suggest at least a year and a half. As we've already shown, this gives puppy love time to either mature into true love or to dissipate. And it gives both people plenty of time to get to know one another and the other person's family.

Most of the time, a person's personality is established early in life. In fact, research shows that *most* people don't change much after the age of six. Although Christians know that with God's help, anybody can change at any age, we also realize that few people choose to do so. They may make minor changes as they grow and mature, but for the most part, a person's personality remains stable. That is why it is so important to take the time to get to know someone before marriage.

We have counseled many engaged people who naively believe that the other person will change after they get married. Then they get upset when we encourage them to wait to be married until they can accept their future spouses as they are, faults and all.

Keep Your Marriage Bed Pure

Statistics show that couples who live together before marriage have a divorce rate more than 70 percent higher than couples who do not.[3] We believe this is because people who demand immediate gratification are less likely to tough it out during the difficult times.

People often like to argue with us over this one, but studies consistently agree that couples who live together before marriage have not only significantly higher divorce rates but also significantly more marital dissatisfaction if they do stay together.

One of the key ingredients in any marriage is trust. But living together and having sexual relations before marriage builds distrust. Your mind doesn't know how to be committed part of the time but not committed the other part. In fact, if everyone, Christian or not, refused to have sex before marriage, we're sure they would find mates who really loved their souls instead of just their bodies.

Fifty percent of men have cheated on their wives. The number of women who cheat on their husbands is close to 40 percent and continues to grow.[4] None of us is safe from this area of temptation. As we will see in chapter 8, the best way to overcome it is to prepare for it. Structure your life so you avoid compromising situations and know how you will respond if you do find yourself tempted.

If you want to experience an unhappy marriage, having an affair is a surefire, money-back-guaranteed way to do it. We have seen the heartbreak that accompanies affairs. Affairs are like premarital sex—the ounce of fun in the beginning is simply not worth the pound of misery in the end. Once you cheat on a spouse, you can never undo it. Spouses do forgive, but they rarely ever forget.

Your mate can give you love, but trust has to be earned over a long period of time. If your significant other cheats on you, repents, and asks for forgiveness, there is a chance that with counseling, the relationship can be healed. But it's difficult to trust that person until she has earned it again. Pay attention to what she does, not what she says. Does she weep over the pain she has caused? Is she willing to see a counselor with you? Has she arranged for a prayer partner or some other form of accountability to help her resist temptation in the future?

Give love. Give forgiveness. But never give trust until it is earned.

Divorce Is Not an Option

As psychiatrists, we regularly deal with suicidal people. Some people spend much of their time thinking about killing themselves. But as long as they focus on whether or not they want to live, they will not get better. It's only when they decide suicide is not an option that they begin to improve. Without that option, they realize they had better start doing what they can to make life better.

The same can be said about divorce. The person who thinks he can always get a divorce if things get bad will spend his time and energy trying to decide if things are bad enough yet for a divorce.

Every marriage will experience hard times. But the person who says "I'm in this marriage for the long haul" can focus his energy on making the marriage better. If you can leave at any time, there's no reason for you to make improvements. When you can't, you are more motivated to make things better.

Every once in a while we see a client who says, "I think I married the wrong person, so what do I do now?" We always respond the same way: Once you say *I do*, your spouse becomes the right person, and you are obligated to make the marriage work.

Of course, divorce is justified in some situations. Jesus says a man can divorce his wife because of adultery (Matthew 5:32; 19:9). Sometimes sharing life with another person becomes impossible, such as in cases of abuse or addiction. In these instances, we usually encourage separation. We have found that separation sometimes causes the abuser to repent and get long-term help, although not always.

Physicians and counselors have known for a long time that divorced people report more depression. Divorce is often more difficult than even the death of a beloved mate, because in divorce, the mate is rejecting you willfully. In the past, psychiatrists assumed that divorce caused depression, and it often does. But newer studies have shown that many divorced people also reported depression preceding the divorce.

When one spouse suffers from depression, marital problems and even divorce often occur, especially if the depression is prolonged. When a spouse is depressed, the partner usually starts out by being sympathetic and trying to help. But if the depression continues, the partner often becomes resentful, especially if she believes the depressed person isn't doing anything to break the cycle of depression. Unfortunately, the depression usually worsens after a divorce.

Every marriage has problems. Turning your back on the problems or ignoring them will only make them worse. Knowing how to communicate is vital to having a happy marriage. Whole books have been written on how to communicate in marriage, and it is much too large a subject to cover here.

What we do want you to know is this: If you and your partner are not able to communicate, get some counseling to help you learn to relate to one another. If you don't, the relationship is guaranteed to deteriorate. Some people, especially men, have a tough time sharing their feelings and need help learning to do so. This is best learned before marriage, but any time is better than none.

The Bottom Line

As you've probably realized by now, who you marry is one of the most significant decisions you will make in life. Good choices in this area will play a key role in your ability to lead a satisfied, enjoyable life.

Bad decisions, which often result from being hasty and ignoring God's leading, will bring misery and regret. If you are unhappy in your current situation, it's probably a clue that something is wrong and that you should do what you can to make the situation better. God wants you to enjoy your work and perform your duties to the best of your ability. God also wants you to enjoy a happy marriage and the rewards of seeking him.

CHAPTER 7

Friends Are Worth Their Weight in Gold

So Become a Millionaire

*Let us endeavor so to live that when we come
to die even the undertaker will be sorry.*

MARK TWAIN

THE TRAGEDY OF PUDD'NHEAD WILSON AND

THE COMEDY OF THE EXTRAORDINARY TWINS

✦

*Good friends, good books and a sleepy
conscience: this is the ideal life.*

MARK TWAIN, "NOTEBOOK," 1898

WAIT A MINUTE, YOU are probably saying, *didn't chapter 2 say that money has little to do with happiness?* Why would we turn around now and say that you should become a millionaire? We're not talking about being a financial millionaire. We're talking about something much more valuable than money; we want you to become a millionaire in friends!

Many of our clients have successful careers, nice homes, and healthy families, but they are still lonely and isolated. What they lack is a close bond with other people. There are usually two reasons for this: They are either too busy, or they don't know how to develop that bond. Yes, some of the friendliest people do not understand how to cultivate close relationships. We don't want you to end up in this situation, so we're going to explore how you can become a millionaire in friends.

The Ultimate Example of Friendship

First, what is a friendship millionaire? Someone who has a million friends? Of course, that's physically impossible. So how many friends should a person have? Let's take a look at Jesus' life. If we would want to emulate any person, it would be Jesus. He had four levels of friends: personal friends, close friends, social friends, and acquaintances.

Personal friends are those people who know everything about you, and you know everything about them. They know your likes, dislikes, dreams, and heartaches. You share their victories and defeats. These are your best friends, your inner circle. Jesus had three personal friends—Peter, James, and John—who were with him throughout his three-year ministry. They accompanied Jesus during some of his most crucial moments on this earth: at the Transfiguration and in the garden of Gethsemane. They knew Jesus better than anyone else on earth.

The rest of the disciples, and possibly Mary Magdalene, fall under the category of close friends. Mary Magdalene was the last person to be with Jesus when he died and the first to see him when he arose, so she held a very significant place in his life. He obviously wanted everyone who read the Gospels to know she was a very important friend.

Jesus' close friends, the other disciples, knew and loved him very much (with the possible exception of Judas Iscariot), and spent a lot of time with him. Jesus confided in them, even though they were not his innermost circle.

Then there were Jesus' social friends, which included Lazarus, Zacchaeus, and many more. These were people who only saw Jesus every once in a while but still cared about him deeply. He loved them; in fact, Jesus wept when Lazarus died, just before he raised him from the dead.

Jesus had many social friends and even more acquaintances with whom he interacted occasionally. He was friendly with his acquaintances but usually did not share his heart with them. In your life, acquaintances might be people at work, people you know from church, people you've met at the gym, or your neighbors.

We don't need to be dogmatic about the number of friends one has. Just because Jesus had three or four personal friends, don't think you have to get rid of one if you have four or five. You don't have to have exactly nine close friends. What is important is having people in every group. The pattern should look like the pyramid below:

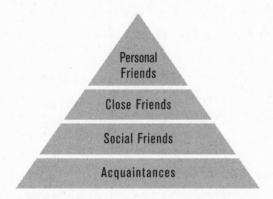

Some people distort the pyramid, having a lot of acquaintances and social friends but no personal or close friends. Some people's lives are so closed off they have very few acquaintances or social friends at all.

Everyone should have at least two or three close friends, people to confide in and even share struggles with. Everyone needs a prayer partner, someone to trust. When you share a burden with a friend like this, you are left with only half of a burden. When you share a sin you struggle with, you will commit that sin less often.

▶ *Paul Meier*

Personal friends are the most difficult to come by, because having a personal friend means exposing your weaknesses. Some people are unwilling to do this. But personal friends really are vital to living a full life. One of the wisest decisions I ever made was to always have a prayer partner—a male friend who knows every secret thought and every sin I commit. *My prayer partner is someone who can keep his mouth shut and someone who has a few sins of his own to confess to me; otherwise I'd be hesitant to share my own struggles.*

In 1975, Dave Larson and I were both psychiatry residents at Duke and were in the same Bible study. Dave and I are both right-brained dreamers who were not typical psych residents. Dave grew up in a well-to-do family in a healthy local church environment, and he had come to feel sorry for those who seemed to be missing out on a personal relationship with God. Dave's dream was to make spirituality palatable to doctors and other academics.

In contrast to Dave, I grew up poor. My mother had little education and cleaned for local doctors. I attended a legalistic church in my early youth, where I was punished for using a pair of scissors on Sunday and not allowed to go to movies or square dance at school. As I grew older, my dream was to love legalists back to health. I wanted to write books that would help legalists become more practical Christians. I wanted to talk to them on the radio and teach future pastors a better way to live.

As we pursued our goals, Dave and I prayed together about everything, including these dreams of ours. And now, thirty years later, half of the medical schools in the United States offer courses to help future doctors understand the value of spirituality in people's lives. Dr. Dave Larson designed those courses. He had such a huge impact on the scientific community's openness to spirituality that a Chair at the Library of Congress (a scholarship given to others with similar pursuits) was named for him.

During those thirty years, I wrote books that sold millions of copies in many languages, and I taught thousands of missionaries and pastors and future pastors all around the world. Dave and I both had setbacks and discouragements along the way that might have caused us to give up our dreams, but because we had each other, our dreams stayed alive.

Dave died a few years ago, and Dr. Jean-Luc Bertrand became my new prayer partner. I also have a few other very close male friends, including my coauthor Todd Clements, with whom I can share anything. I do have some trusted female friends, but neither Todd nor I recommend that you have a best friend—the prayer partner type—of the opposite sex. Such an intimate relationship makes it all too easy to cross the line into an affair. I know that Jesus had Mary Magdalene as a close friend, and Jesus was without sin—though, according to the Bible, he was tempted to sin just as we are. But I don't claim to be Jesus.

For several years, we have studied patterns among people who make and keep friends and those who don't, and together we have come to the following conclusions.

The Wrong Way to Make Friends

Trying to impress people

Trying to impress people into liking you rarely ever works. Men are the worst at this. We think if we're smart enough, handsome enough, athletic enough, social enough, or rich enough, people will like us. In our quest to win others, we forget the main ingredient: caring.

If you want to make friends, stop trying to impress people and instead allow them to impress you. How do you do that? Begin by asking about them and caring about their lives. When others talk, especially about themselves, the tendency is to tune them out and think, *What am I going to say next?* Or even, *How can my story beat this?* But instead of preparing your response, concentrate on the significance of what the other person is saying. Human beings are just like living novels, each with many interesting stories, gifts, and abilities to be discovered.

Much of a psychiatrist's workday is spent listening to others. People tell us about their lives for a whole hour, while we say little in return. We often hear compliments such as "You're a great conversationalist" or "I really enjoy talking with you," when we've said almost nothing. The secret is that we show interest in the lives of our clients. It's worth noting that these people come to us to learn something, but we also learn a great deal by listening to them. We learn about different cultures, businesses, religions, and ways of life. If you want to impress people with your intelligence, listen to what they have to say. Not only will you seem smarter, you will actually become smarter.

The old proverb attributed to Confucius rings true: "God created you with two ears and only one mouth because he wanted you to listen more than talk."

Waiting for others to take the initiative

"Well, I try to make friends all the time, but it just doesn't work."

We hear that statement all too often. And when we ask for a specific example, the answer usually shows a halfhearted, feeble attempt at gaining a friend. What many people consider trying to make friends is actually little more than sitting around waiting for someone to call. In order to really develop a relationship, you need to take the initiative and call others.

When we ask people in their teens, twenties, or even early thirties how many close friends they have—friends who know their secrets and love them anyway—those clients look at us like we must be crazy. Then they almost always respond, "Are you kidding? Are there really people like that?"

The way our society is set up, people of higher social standing usually initiate contact with those of lower social standing. For instance, you would not normally ask your boss out for dinner; it would be up to him to ask you. But we want to challenge you to be brave and think outside of the box. We're not saying you should call the president and tell him you're spending the night at the White House, but don't be afraid to approach others.

One good method of getting out of the box is to participate in two different social hobbies, such as playing golf, working out, scrapbooking, or participating in a cooking club. Find others who share your hobby, ask them about it, and encourage them to join you in it.

Practicing "empty talk"

▶ *Todd Clements*

I grew up on a farm in Arkansas, where we watched the weather closely. A beautiful sunny afternoon might change in the blink of an eye. I learned to look out in the western sky and see a faint gray on the horizon accompanied by barely audible rumblings of faraway thunder. Within an hour the sky would be black and the thunder at sonic boom levels, shaking the ground with each crack. We all switched into high gear during these times. A sudden storm dumping a downpour could wreak havoc on our crops if we were not prepared to quickly cut holes in dikes or dig ditches in the fields. Whenever we saw a storm approaching, my dad would hop in his truck to check the fields while the rest of us readied the tractors. He radioed back which fields needed draining, and we scurried to get it done.

Most storms did not flood our farmland, and the majority brought much-needed rainfall. On occasion, the clouds actually brought nothing. These times were extremely frustrating. Filled with thunder and lightning like a rainstorm, they brought only wind. They left behind only disappointment after blowing through without providing vital rain. Today, however, these clouds can't fool us as we are "high-tech rednecks" and have a radar system in place.

"Empty talk" is much like those clouds. In fact the Bible compares hollow words to rainless clouds: "Like clouds and wind without rain is a man who boasts of gifts he does not give" (Proverbs 25:14).

Empty talk is making statements you don't intend to fulfill, as when you say to somebody, "Hey, let's go eat sometime," or "I'll call you," with no real intention of actually ever following through. Even if you are only trying to be nice, it is still frustrating to the other person when he or she realizes that you never meant what you said. People who don't follow through with what they say are hard to trust. And people don't want to make friends with someone they cannot trust. If you make a statement, think of it as an obligation and do everything in your power to carry it out.

The Right Way to Make Friends

Since we knew it all, we've learned that there are some foundational steps to building productive friendships. The first is recognizing that building friendships takes time, energy, and effort. Contrary to popular belief, good friendships don't just happen. Those who want friends must show themselves friendly—in other words, friends have to be earned.

Buy a big calendar

Buy yourself a calendar even if you have a photographic memory. Why? Because it will help you to remember your friends' birthdays and anniversaries. Good friends keep up with dates that are important to other people. This requires a little effort on your part, although today PDAs and computers do make it easier to keep track of important dates.

I (Dr. Clements) always carry a pen and a piece of paper with me. Countless times a day, I make notes to myself and write down important events. It could be a birthday I want to remember or promotions at work, the anniversary of a loved one's death, or other important dates.

But just keeping track of important dates in your friends' lives isn't enough. You also have to acknowledge them. You might make a phone call or send an e-mail or personal note. People always appreciate handwritten cards because they show that you care enough to spend time writing them. I have a designated time each Sunday night where I sit down and write cards or letters and plan any phone calls for the upcoming week. This takes some work, but it is very rewarding and pays off one-hundred-fold.

Be prudent in keeping secrets

As psychiatrists, we are often asked to keep secrets. And being able to keep a secret is also an important part of true friendship. But we also have to be judicious in the way we handle secrets. The mishandling of confidential information can ruin relationships.

Sometimes, the more secrets you know, the easier it is to let one slip. For instance, let's say you're friends with Karen and Jane. Jane's boyfriend Matt has been secretly calling Karen, and Karen tells you, asking you to keep this a secret from Jane. Now you're in a precarious situation. What if you forget and let something slip? Then Karen is upset with you. What if Jane finds out about the whole ordeal and realizes that you knew all the time and never told her? Then she's angry with you. It's a no-win situation.

Sometimes the best way to handle a secret is to tell people up front, "I'm no good at keeping secrets, so if you know something that can't be repeated and you tell me, it's at your own risk." This puts the ball in their court. But if they choose to tell you their secret anyway, it's important that you take it seriously and do all that you can to protect that confidence.

Be willing to forgive

Have you ever gotten mad at a friend before and decided to write him or her off? A lot of people do that. But before long they've written off all their friends and either have to make new ones or go back and rekindle relationships with the old ones. Here's a good saying to remember: "Friends will lift you up and let you down." Friends will make you mad, sad, and glad. They will disappoint you at times, and you'll do the same thing to them. Most of us have trouble realizing how we could disappoint someone else or make another person mad, but we do.

The apostle Peter had trouble with friends letting him down. In fact, he asked Jesus, "Lord, how often should I forgive someone who sins against me? Seven times?"

Jesus answered, "No, not seven times, but seventy times seven!" (Matthew 18:21-22, NLT). The rabbis—the religious leaders of that time—taught that someone should be forgiven three times, then written off after that. Peter thought he was being generous by agreeing to forgive up to seven times. No doubt Jesus' answer floored Peter. Taken literally, seventy times seven is four hundred and ninety. Most people understand this verse to mean Jesus wants us to forgive others as many times as needed. Paradoxically, it's often our friends who require the most forgiveness.

Forgiving is so important that Jesus said if we don't forgive others, God won't forgive us.

> **For if you forgive men when they sin against you, your heavenly Father will also forgive you. But if you do not forgive men their sins, your Father will not forgive your sins.** MATTHEW 6:14-15

Listen carefully to the words of the Lord's Prayer the next time you recite it. You are asking God to "forgive us for our sins as much as we forgive those who sin against us." Forgiveness is more for our benefit than that of the person we are forgiving. Forgiving another person may have little or no effect on his or her life, but it will make all the difference to yours. Unforgiveness is a poison that will eat your life away.

In our practices, we often see people who have experienced horrific tragedies in their lives. Some are able to put the tragedy behind them and move on to live happy, meaningful lives. But others remain depressed, unhappy, and anxiety ridden. What's the difference? Most often it is due to bitterness—a lack of forgiveness.

▶ *Paul Meier*

Those we don't forgive we become enslaved to. One of my patients, Helen, suffered depression after a drunk driver killed her son. She thought about the wreck 24-7 and talked incessantly about it, running most of her friends off as a result. The drunk driver involved in the wreck received only proba- tion, which infuriated Helen. She made it her mission to catch this guy violating probation, so she spent her days armed with a camera, parked outside of his apartment, trying to catch him drinking a beer or doing something else that might send him to jail. Each week as she agonized over her countless hours of unfruitful labor, I suggested forgiving this man.

She would have none of it. Her answer was, "I don't feel like I can ever forgive him," and as far as I know she never did. The last time I brought up the subject of forgiving him, she became angry and said, "I'm not interested in forgiving him because I can never forget what he has done to me. Besides, I'm seeing you to get some pills to help me feel better, not to try to convince me to forgive this animal." Sadly, I don't know of any pills that can completely overcome unforgiveness.

Helen had several major misconceptions about forgiveness. The first was that you have to feel like forgiving someone in order to do it. On the contrary, forgiveness is a choice we make, and most of the time we don't ever feel like doing it. Also our forgiveness cannot hinge on whether the other person asks for it. Jesus never even mentioned the other person's response in his command for us to forgive.

Just because we forgive someone doesn't mean we must forget what that person did to us. That's not humanly possible. Now God does have the power to forgive and forget. His Word promises, "As far as the east is from the west, so far has he removed our transgressions from us" (Psalm 103:12). But we don't have that same power, nor have we been asked to forget. In fact, remembering a transgression is often a protection to keep it from happening again. If you want to be a millionaire in friends, you will have to be a billionaire in forgiveness. But that's what God calls us to do anyway.

Have friends outside your family

Tight-knit families are wonderful, especially since many problems in our society today spring from the unraveling of the close family ties that characterized past generations. But it is still important to have friends who are not family members. There is no hard rule or commandment in the Scriptures on this subject, but there are some commonsense reasons to cultivate outside friendships.

It's not wise to view one of your parents as your best friend. An astute parent will realize this and encourage you to seek other friends. When a mom and daughter are too close, it's common for the mom to rule the relationship and even manipulate the daughter. While it's good to be friends with your mother, you must be careful that she's not overly involved in your life. If you find yourself talking to your mom for more than an hour every day, consider taking a step back in order to allow room for outside relationships.

A father can also become too involved in his child's life. If you find yourself answering to your dad rather than your spouse, the relationship is too close. The Bible is pretty clear on this point: "For this reason a man will leave his father and mother and be united to his wife, and they will become one flesh" (Genesis 2:24).

Enjoy the relationship you have with your family, but work to cultivate other friends as well. Friends offer a different perspective on life. They like you because of who you are, not because they're related to you!

Be open but not petty

We all know people who get upset if somebody looks at them cross-eyed. These people do not do well with friendships. And most of us do not like to be around them because we're constantly worried and wondering if we've done something to hurt their feelings.

The word *petty* means trivial or insignificant. People who are petty constantly ride others with guilt, focusing on all the insignificant things they see as wrong.

In reality, pettiness is false humility, which is a form of pride. False humility comes in two forms. First, petty people constantly make derogatory statements about themselves in front of others. This is actually an effort to force others to build them up (although the people who do this always deny that's why they do it).

Petty people also practice a second form of false humility by assuming that others are constantly thinking about them. Psychiatry has invented a word for this phenomena—personalization, believing everything that happens somehow involves you.

I (Dr. Meier) had a female patient who started crying in my office because I supposedly ignored her in an office supply store, proving I did not like her. She said she had waved at me while I was looking right at her, and I did not return the wave or speak. Actually, I didn't have my contacts in or glasses on at the time, so I'm sure the only thing I saw was a blur. It had nothing at all to do with her. This woman never did learn that everything was not about her, and she continues to go through life with onion-thin skin.

The most well-adjusted people today are those who have thick skin and a warm heart. They don't get caught up in insignificant matters or pettiness. They know that doing so will ruin good relationships.

If a friend hurts your feelings, be open about it. There is nothing worse than remaining angry yet refusing to tell the person why you are angry. It's unfair to expect someone to read your mind.

▶ *Todd Clements*

A guy in my college dormitory loved to play jokes. His room was directly above the side entrance, and his favorite prank was to pour a bucket of water on people as they were return- ing to the dorm. We had to walk right under his window and punch in a combination for the door to open, which always took a few seconds. He especially liked to get people when they were dressed up.

One Friday evening several of us were drinking soda pop and hanging out on the upper patio, which overlooks the parking lot. We watched as a well-dressed guy headed to his car to pick up a date. It was the guy who liked to play jokes! We had all been drenched by this guy numerous times, so I stood up and threw a can of pop from the upper patio all the way across the parking lot, where it landed about ten feet from him. The can exploded on impact, drenching him from head to toe. Those of us on the patio gave each other high fives as the shower of fizzy pop could not have been more perfectly placed. (I don't recommend trying this at home, as throwing soda cans at another person is, in retrospect, pretty dumb.)

The guy laughed about it and came back in to change clothes, and we all made a truce to quit throwing liquids on each other.

*But later that week, Larry, another one of my dorm buddies,
started giving me the cold shoulder. I finally asked him if he was
mad at me for some reason, and he said, "Don't worry about it."
So I didn't. Come to find out, however, the guy I drenched with
pop had been wearing Larry's shirt that night. Larry told another
guy that he couldn't believe I would have such total disregard
for his expensive shirt, especially since he was not rich.*

*Larry's reaction was problematic for a number of reasons.
First, Larry was personalizing an event that had nothing to
do with him. No one had any clue that was Larry's shirt,
nor meant any harm to him. Second, his anger was somewhat petty too, since the shirt could easily be washed. Finally,
although Larry told everybody else he was mad at me, he
didn't tell me directly. As soon as I found out, I insisted on
paying for the shirt to be cleaned, pressed, and starched.
Larry could have saved himself a lot of angry feelings and
me a lot of confusion if he had just been direct.*

In the New Testament, we are urged repeatedly to speak the truth in love,
and in Ephesians 4:26-27, we are told to get angry without sinning, but
to get rid of that anger by bedtime. If you hang on to your anger, you give
Satan a foothold in your life, because he loves to turn your bitterness
toward God, others, or even toward yourself.

The Bible always encourages us to go to the other person. Do not
wait for the other person to come to you like Larry did. The other person
may not even realize he has hurt you. Our natural inclination, however,
is to tell other people first in an attempt to garner their sympathy. Jesus
clearly describes the right way to handle such situations:

> **If your brother sins against you, go and show him his fault,
> just between the two of you. If he listens to you, you have won
> your brother over.** MATTHEW 18:15

The verses following this one describe what to do if this first step does not work, but usually going directly to the offended person will take care of the matter.

In the Old Testament laws, the Jews were told to share their anger with their neighbors without getting vengeful (Leviticus 19:17). This openness always keeps matters from getting blown out of proportion.

The Bottom Line

Entire books have been written on the subject of friendship. We hope this chapter at least scratches the surface enough to help you realize how important it is to make and cultivate ongoing relationships.

Maybe you've been unconsciously employing some of the wrong tactics mentioned. The good news is you can turn them around anytime. Making friends is a lifelong endeavor.

Research proves that people who have strong bonds with others live the happiest, healthiest lives. Isolation leads to discouragement and depression. So set your mind to make good solid friendships, and start by being a good friend. Remember that the work you put into friendships will pay off. Be open with your friends and never stop forgiving them.

CHAPTER 8

You Will Face Temptation

So Learn to Walk the Other Way

[Temptation] is easier to stay out than get out.

MARK TWAIN, PUDD'NHEAD WILSON'S NEW CALENDAR, *FOLLOWING THE EQUATOR*

✦

*There are several good protections against
temptation, but the surest is cowardice.*

MARK TWAIN, PUDD'NHEAD WILSON'S NEW CALENDAR, *FOLLOWING THE EQUATOR*

I **(DR. CLEMENTS) ONCE TOOK** an unscientific poll of an audience, asking how many people there would like to live a sin-free life. All 216 people raised their hands. If the desire to live sin free is so unanimous, the plan should be simple enough: Don't give in to temptation. But following that plan isn't easy, as everybody knows.

Temptation to sin is an inescapable fact of life, and we all fail from time to time. Since the fall of Adam and Eve, every human is prone to sin. Genesis 8:21 says of man: "Every inclination of his heart is evil from childhood." But God wants to teach us how to overcome sin because of the destructiveness it reaps in our lives.

Temptation itself is not sin. Jesus was tempted, although he never sinned. Temptations are enticements and allurements to fulfill fleshly desires contrary to the loving, moral, and righteous life God chooses for us. Temptations come not only from Satan but also from our own love of the world's pleasures. Sin occurs when we give in to the temptation.

In this chapter we will reveal the first, fundamental step you can take to help yourself become victorious over temptation. Those who master this step usually go on to lead productive and satisfying lives. Those who don't can become enslaved to certain sins, resulting in roller-coaster lives.

The best way to beat temptation is to simply walk away from it! We'll explain how to do that in several areas, starting with one of the most difficult: sexual temptation.

Temptation and Sex

Sexual temptation remains the major struggle for adolescents and young adults today. Though sex in itself is good, and God created it for a reason, he did put boundaries on it. Sex is reserved for marriage between a male and a female.

In Proverbs we read, "Rejoice in the wife of your youth.... May her breasts satisfy you always, may you ever be captivated by her love" (Proverbs 5:18-19). From these verses, it's clear that God created sex for our pleasure. And if you think this passage is a little wild, wait until you read what God said in the Song of Solomon, a book that is an example of the physical union between two married lovers and also an illustration of the spiritual love between God and each of us.

While sex within God's boundaries is positive, violating God's direction to avoid sex outside of marriage can have serious and lasting consequences. Though we've changed the names, the story that follows is a true one—a profoundly sad example of what can happen when a young person gives in to temptation.

▶ *Todd Clements*

Seventeen-year-old Cynthia was pregnant. An honor student and acclaimed cheerleader, she was the last person anyone would have expected to be in this situation. But Cynthia had been secretly dating Jason, a twenty-year-old local guy who was still trying to decide what to do with his life.

Cynthia broke the news of her pregnancy to her mother on the way home from a summer cheerleading camp. She told about her secret relationship with Jason and their plans to marry. Her parents, Sharon and Jake, were embarrassed, but more than that, they were worried for their daughter. Her boyfriend did not even have a job. How would their daughter finish school? What about college? Who would support them? How would they tell the grandparents? How would they explain this to their younger children?

Cynthia had hoped to cheer for football season, but sickness related to her pregnancy interfered. Her dreams of cheerleading in college or even going to college at all were dashed.

Cynthia had three reasonable options for her future. She could have the baby but not marry Jason, at least until she had known him longer. We do not believe getting pregnant somehow spiritually obligates two people to marry each other. In fact, if one person is a Christian and the other isn't, we will advise the Christian not to marry the non-Christian.

A second option was that Cynthia could have the baby, give it up to a good Christian adoption agency, and go on to fulfill her dreams of cheerleading, going to college, dating, and eventually marrying.

Third, Cynthia could decide she really loved Jason enough to marry him, and hope for the best. She chose the third door, which turned out to be the wrong one in her case. She had serious doubts about marrying Jason, but she did not know what else to do. Her father decided that if she was old enough to get pregnant, then she was old enough to take care of herself. He agreed to pay for the wedding but refused to support her and Jason.

Jason felt he was portrayed as the bad guy and was convinced Cynthia's family did not like him. Thinking of the responsibility that comes with supporting a family brought on panic attacks and nausea. He was ambivalent about getting married and settling down with one girl for the rest of his life but felt it was the honorable thing to do.

Cynthia had dreamed of a summer evening wedding in her church ever since she was a little girl. Now she was too embarrassed to even have a public wedding, opting instead for a family-only ceremony. The couple had a healthy baby girl. We wish the story had a happily-ever-after ending, but here's real life. A large construction company hired Jason and sent him to Mexico to help with a dam-building project. There he met a local girl and had an affair. He then divorced Cynthia, renounced his United States citizenship, and has lived in Mexico ever since.

Since Jason is neither a U.S. citizen nor a resident of this country, Cynthia has been unable to make him pay any kind of alimony or child support. To this day he has no contact with their daughter.

Cynthia's family appropriately stepped up to the plate when she was abandoned by Jason and chose to help her through the ordeal. She is in college now, and Sharon keeps her granddaughter while Cynthia goes to class and works.

Though Cynthia has been getting along and likes college,

she finds it hard to meet new guys because most of them are not interested in a girl with a baby. Cynthia's biggest regret is giving in to the sexual temptation with Jason. She says, "If I had only known then what I know now, life would be different."

In a counseling session before he went to Mexico, Jason was asked if he had advice for other guys. He said, "I sure do. The few minutes of pleasure I got from having sex with Cynthia is not worth what I am going through now. A hundred times the pleasure would not be worth it. Sexual desire is only gratified for a short while, because in an hour you're right back to feeling the way you did before, but the consequences can last a lifetime."

You may think Cynthia could have avoided her problems if she had simply used birth control, but birth control is not completely reliable. In fact, Jason *had* been using protection.

Some readers may believe the couple could have kept the pregnancy secret and simply gotten an abortion. But in our practice, we have found that the consequences of post-abortion syndrome are much worse than the consequences of having the child. We believe abortion is the taking of a human life.

Sadly, we could write a whole book on people whose lives have been ruined by the improper use of sex. We have both counseled men and women who are HIV positive because of illicit sex. They come to us at nineteen years old, knowing they may never live to see thirty.

Proverbs warns that if we have extramarital sex, our bodies might wither away and die as a result: "At the end of your life you will groan, when your flesh and body are spent" (Proverbs 5:11). HIV is just one of dozens of sexually transmitted diseases. Condoms can make contracting these diseases less likely, but that is all they can do. Many diseases, including AIDS, can be transmitted even if the man is wearing double condoms every time. We always warn our patients that even with precaution, one out of six will still get the disease. These are the same odds as playing Russian roulette with a six-shooting revolver. Another sexually transmitted disease, herpes, is especially troublesome because there is no cure for it. And one out of four adult Americans has it.

As in the case of Cynthia and Jason, unwanted pregnancies are rampant because of sexual relations outside of God's boundaries. Nothing can ruin a future faster than an unplanned pregnancy. The birth of an unplanned child to teenagers who are in the prime of their lives—making friends, preparing for the future, and having fun—forces them to accept the responsibility of parenthood and marriage before they are ready. Even if the couple is ready to get married, they are often not ready for a child immediately. Statistics show that having a baby in the first two years of marriage increases a couple's chance for divorce. (But having a baby after two years actually lowers the chances.) Marriages need time to grow as each partner gets to know the other.

Unplanned pregnancies affect not only the mother and the father but both extended families too. We see an increase in depression and anxiety in the parents and siblings of the mother- and father-to-be. An illegitimate pregnancy also places a social stigma on both families involved.

The magnitude of sexual temptation for young people today is no surprise given the number of contributing factors. First, teenagers' bodies are going through a revolution. Adolescence ushers in high testosterone levels, turning boys into men. Girls also experience a testosterone surge along with increased estrogen, forming the body and mind of a woman. These hormonal changes leave young adults with high sexual desire, especially young men.

At the same time the mind is experiencing sexual cravings, something else is happening. Adolescence brings in new freedoms. High schoolers start driving. This leads to dating, which leads to intimate situations with the opposite sex. Now we're not saying that girls and guys in high school should never be together alone. This would only make the problem worse later. But young men and women have to learn to make wise decisions regarding sex.

Our society has tremendous influence on these hormonally aroused bodies and minds that now have more freedom with the opposite sex than ever before. Television and movies inundate us with sexual scenarios that fall outside the boundaries drawn by God. Magazine headlines scream from grocery checkout stands: "Seven new secrets to better sex!" And popular music is filled with innuendo and blatant sexuality.

Obviously, we aren't saying you should live as a hermit and disassociate from society. But you do need to know and understand the truth about sexual temptation and the way that culture influences these passions. Remember, sexual temptation itself is not a sin.

God's Word offers a great example of resisting sexual temptation in the story of Joseph:

> Now Joseph was well-built and handsome, and after a while his master's wife took notice of Joseph and said, "Come to bed with me!" But he refused. . . . And though she spoke to Joseph day after day, he refused to go to bed with her or even be with her.
>
> One day he went into the house to attend to his duties, and none of the household servants was inside. She caught him by his cloak and said, "Come to bed with me!" But he left his cloak in her hand and ran out of the house.   GENESIS 39:6-12

Joseph refused to place himself in any situation that could be compromising. Female clients tell us how they sometimes spend the night with their boyfriends but nothing happens, even though they sleep in the same bed. That's no different than playing with fire and expecting not to get burned. If you are serious about staying pure, why allow yourself to be in that situation?

The Temptations of Drugs and Drinking

Drugs and alcohol provide another major temptation for young adults. Our flesh longs for these substances because they bring us pleasure—at first. (See a detailed discussion in chapter 9.) However, drug use also guarantees numerous consequences. Though cocaine, methamphetamines, and marijuana were not available in biblical times, alcohol was, and the book of Proverbs has several things to say concerning alcohol:

> Wine is a mocker and beer a brawler; whoever is led astray by them is not wise. —PROVERBS 20:1

> He who loves pleasure will become poor; whoever loves wine and oil will never be rich. —PROVERBS 21:17

> Listen, my son, and be wise, and keep your heart on the right path. Do not join those who drink too much wine or gorge themselves on meat, for drunkards and gluttons become poor, and drowsiness clothes them in rags. —PROVERBS 23:19-21

> Who has woe? Who has sorrow? Who has strife? Who has complaints? Who has needless bruises? Who has bloodshot eyes? Those who linger over wine, who go to sample bowls of mixed wine. Do not gaze at wine when it is red, when it sparkles in the cup, when it goes down smoothly! In the end it bites like a snake and poisons like a viper. —PROVERBS 23:29-32

Is it a sin to take a drink of alcohol? No. In fact, Jesus' first miracle involved his changing water into wine at a wedding, and the wedding guests said the host must have saved the best wine for last.

There are a wide variety of beliefs about alcohol even in the Christian community. As psychiatrists, we know that the highest alcoholism rate among religions occurs in those that totally forbid it. The lowest rate of alcoholism is among Jewish people, who traditionally teach their thirteen-year-old sons and daughters after bar mitzvah and bat mitzvah to take a sip with dinner. A brilliant Jewish surgeon once commented to me (Dr.

Meier) that Jewish kids aren't usually tempted to rebel by drinking too much alcohol. "We rebel," he joked, "by not becoming doctors."

We think it is best to stick to the rules that are clear in Scripture, and parents should not be too strict or too lenient when raising children, because either extreme can increase a child's temptation level. It is illegal to drink alcohol in the United States if you are under twenty-one. Smoking is illegal if you are under eighteen, and drugs are illegal all the time. The New Testament is quite clear on our responsibility to obey the law.

> **Everyone must submit to governing authorities. For all authority comes from God, and those in positions of authority have been placed there by God. So anyone who rebels against authority is rebelling against what God has instituted, and they will be punished.** ROMANS 13:1-2, NLT

It is vitally important to know what one's personal convictions are about alcohol. We encourage people to honestly search their hearts and decide what is right and what is wrong for themselves. Write these convictions down on paper so you will have them in black and white (e.g., I will not drink alcohol; I believe it is okay for me to have one glass of wine; etc.), and then when temptation comes, you'll know very easily what your boundaries are.

The Temptation of Being Too Busy

Many other forms of temptation are more subtle than drug and alcohol abuse. One temptation affecting almost all Americans today is busyness. There's an old saying that if the devil can't make you bad, he will make you busy. He's doing that in many of our lives.

Schools today have so many extracurricular activities and so much homework that starting in middle school, some students "work" more hours than a person with a full-time job. Parents often feel like hired chauffeurs, constantly hauling students to and from activities. Students are so busy studying math and science, they have no time to study God's Word and no time to figure out who they are and what they believe.

Placing activities before God is idolatry, even if the activities are good. Take an inventory of your life. Are you too busy? If so what can you cut out? If you stay too busy, the very activities you are doing for pleasure will actually have the opposite effect and begin to rob your life of joy and peace.

When I (Dr. Meier) was ten years old, I decided to read my Bible every day, and I still do this today, fifty years later. If I ever miss it, I really miss it, like missing a meal. I hope to learn to love more deeply the older I get. How could I possibly do this without regularly meditating on God's love letter to us, the Bible?

This may sound crazy, but one hint that your life may be too busy is a difficulty enjoying downtime. It's easy to become addicted to activities, and then we don't know what to do if we don't have some form of activity every minute of the day. You see this in people who talk on the phone all the time or watch numerous TV shows every night. They don't like to be alone because they don't know who they are. They are also afraid of getting in touch with their loneliness and other emotions. Therefore they are always seeking to fill the empty spaces with entertainment, socializing, and pleasure.

The Temptation of Money

The temptation of wealth, which used to be more common among adults, has now infiltrated the teen years. A busy sixteen-year-old came in to see me (Dr. Clements) a couple of weeks ago, complaining of depression. I suggested that rather than antidepressants, she needed to take a break from her grueling class schedule and spend some free time hanging out with friends and having more fun. She explained that this was impossible; she had to start early in order to be accepted to a good medical or law school.

Since medicine and law seemed to be very different career paths,

I asked why she wanted to be a lawyer or a physician. She answered that the earning potential of these two professions would be stable even in economic downtimes.

Here's what Proverbs says about acquiring riches: "Do not wear yourself out to get rich; have the wisdom to show restraint" (Proverbs 23:4).

Wealth is not wrong, but giving your whole life to obtain wealth is. We see miserable wealthy people every day in our offices. Millions of people in this country are working jobs they don't enjoy, living in places they don't want to live, and hanging out with people they do not like. Why? Because they are chasing wealth.

That sixteen-year-old client did not really care about being a physician or a lawyer. She just wanted to be wealthy. Her desire to be rich in the future was ruining her life in the present.

God uses money but not in the way that we use it. We value money because of what it will do *for* us. God uses money to see what it will do *to* us. One of the most heinous dishonesties the world has led us to believe is that money will bring happiness and contentment. This is all smoke and mirrors. Money has very little to do with happiness and nothing at all in common with contentment. Until we understand that happiness and contentment do not come from money, we will always be tempted by it.

> No one can serve two masters. Either he will hate the one and love the other, or he will be devoted to the one and despise the other. You cannot serve both God and Money. MATTHEW 6:24

We must keep our vision clear. We need to enjoy what God gives us, while at the same time understanding that material things are only temporary. Investments can be devalued by inflation. Possessions can be destroyed by natural disasters or stolen by thieves. The person who does not realize that money is fleeting, temporary, and unfulfilling will become enslaved. And that enslaved person, often without even realizing it, then begins to serve money rather than God.

> **Your heavenly Father already knows all your needs. Seek the Kingdom of God above all else, and live righteously, and he will give you everything you need.**   MATTHEW 6:32-33, NLT

Jesus asks us to live right in God's eyes today. God will then take care of our needs for tomorrow. This takes faith to carry out. It's tempting to take our eyes off God and start looking around us at those whose eyes are on material things, especially those who are prosperous. But as Jesus taught, riches on this earth are not secure; only riches in heaven are.

We encourage you to seek God's will for your life, because he knows your gifts and talents and desires, and he loves you and wants what is best for you in the long run. Pray for his wisdom and guidance about your future, no matter how old you are.

The Temptation to Look Down on Others

Sexual sins are indeed harmful to others, and they make God's Top Ten list (the Ten Commandments), but they don't make his Top Seven list. In Proverbs 6:16-19, King Solomon lists the seven sins that God hates the most. Number one on that list is "a proud look" (KJV).

A proud look could be defined as looking down on another human being as though you were better than that person. This includes a lot of things: being racist or sexist, hating all Yankees (or Southerners), thinking you are more spiritual than someone else, looking down on fat (or thin) people, blaming your parents for your imperfections, ignoring those who aren't in your own particular social or religious circle, judging those who struggle with addictions, hating cheerleaders (or noncheerleaders), thinking less of the poor (or the rich), feeling superior to someone with a lower IQ, talking down to a person who suffers from mental illness, pulling rank on those with less power (spouses, children, employees, etc.), or thinking of Democrats (or Republicans) as the "bad guys." As you can see, we've probably all been guilty of giving that proud look at one time or another.

It's very tempting to think we are more important than someone else or some other group of people. Many churches never confront people for this sin. In fact, some churches even encourage this way of thinking.

But if you really want to make God mad, just start thinking you're better than someone else—anyone else. The Bible says that when Jesus comes back to rule the earth for a thousand years (Revelation 20), he is going to completely change the way we view order and hierarchy, making the first to be last and the last to be first. Those who are most despised now will be rulers then. And those who think they're near the top now will be sweeping the floors of the new rulers then.

When God, Creator of all things, decided to become a human, he was born in a manger as the son of a carpenter in the small town of Bethlehem. As an adult, he took off his outer garments and got into his "shorts," getting down on his hands and knees to wash the feet of his friends. He submitted himself to being spat upon, beaten, and crucified on a cross. So when you pray and ask Jesus to make you more like him, be sure you understand that you are requesting him to help you become a really good and humble servant who looks down on nobody and treats every human with dignity.

As you ask God to show you how to walk away from temptations, begin by asking him to show you your secret sins—the ones accepted by your culture that you don't even realize you are committing.

The Truth about Temptation

God knows that as long as we are on this earth, we will face temptation every day. Even if we were to live in a monastery or a convent, we'd still struggle with temptation. But thankfully, God has provided for that.

> **No temptation has seized you except what is common to man. And God is faithful; he will not let you be tempted beyond what you can bear. But when you are tempted, he will also provide a way out so that you can stand up under it.**
>
> 1 CORINTHIANS 10:13

This verse is reassuring, but it can also be misused. One female college student confided in me (Dr. Clements) that she was having trouble in the area of sexual temptation. She admitted she had been secretly spending most nights with her boyfriend in his dorm room, and sometimes they engaged in sex.

"Well a good start would be to stop spending the night there or getting into his bed," I told her. She responded that according to this verse in Corinthians, she should be able to sleep with her boyfriend without succumbing to sexual temptation. But that is not what this verse is implying at all.

Temptation is like every other area of life. God does not do for us what we can do for ourselves, but instead he does for us what we cannot do for ourselves. We should never use this verse as a license to sin.

The key to resisting temptation is strengthening your relationship with Jesus. I (Dr. Meier) pray every morning before my feet hit the floor, *God, help me to become more like you today, especially in the area of love. Help me to serve you, and show your love to others through me. Help me to resist temptations, because you know how easy it is for me to give in to them. And help me to learn and grow from any trials and disappointments that may come my way.*

Later on, I pray for other people on my list, but this is what I always pray first. If the whole day goes by and nothing goes wrong, I consider it to be a "bonus" day. But when things do go wrong, I don't get very upset because I expect to have tests and disappointments, and I expect to become more like Jesus as a result of handling them.

Defining what you believe and what your boundaries are will help you deal with temptation. When you do fail, however, God is never surprised. He knows you inside and out, and he loves you and simply wants you to learn from your failures. The apostle James says that we all fail in many ways (James 3:2). The apostle John says that if anyone tells you he doesn't ever sin anymore, he is only fooling himself and doesn't know the truth (1 John 1:8). The apostle Paul was the greatest evangelist who ever lived, and yet he talked about his failures: not doing what he should and sometimes doing what he shouldn't (Romans 6–7). But Paul also gives us Romans 8:1: "Therefore, there is now no condemnation for those who are in Christ Jesus."

If you were teaching your one-year-old infant to walk and she took a couple of good steps and fell down, would you condemn, shame, and punish her for falling? Of course not, unless you are an absolute tyrant. You might be momentarily sad that she got hurt, but you would delight in that infant and lift her up and hug her and reassure her and hope that she had learned from this fall. And maybe next time, she might even take three or four steps before falling.

When we yield to temptation, God loves us like a parent loves a child, and he is sad when we get hurt falling. Yet he delights in us, lifts us up, and reassures us that we all fall in many ways. He tells us there is no condemnation for falling if we have trusted in him. His blood paid for every one of our falls already. We owe nothing.

We serve God, not to earn our way to heaven—which is impossible anyway—but because we love and appreciate him. We understand that there is nothing more meaningful than this. In fact, do you know what God calls someone who fails seven times but keeps getting back up and learning from his failures? A righteous person (Proverbs 24:16).

That answer surprises many of our clients. So many people have learned to be self-condemning from a parent who was never quite satisfied. But if you are a seven-time loser, congratulations—God sees you as a righteous person as long as you don't give up. Don't ever expect to be perfect, because that won't happen until heaven. But don't give up on your quest to becoming a better lover of God, others, and yourself. In fact, that verse says someone who fails only once and gives up is an unrighteous person.

Every sin hurts somebody. That is why God calls them sins. He doesn't want us to go around hurting people, and he doesn't want us to get hurt either. So the more we learn to love and be loved, the easier it will be to walk away from temptations to hurt other people or ourselves.

Is this starting to make sense yet? The less we experience the feeling of being deeply loved and deeply loving in return, the less significant we feel, and the easier it is for Satan to tempt us with various lusts of the flesh (food, drugs, sex), lusts of the eyes (money, material possessions), and the pride of life (power, control, prestige).

Unfortunately, some religious groups today try to make us think that illicit sex is the only sin, or at least the worst sin. But in doing so, they overlook all the other sins we all so easily commit. It is so easy to become self-righteous and condemn other people while overlooking our own sinfulness. Sometimes we have to experience multiple failures before we realize that we need others—maybe even a professional Christian counselor—to help us overcome sin and temptation.

The Bottom Line

In Psalm 139, David says that our loving God designed you in your mother's womb, he thought about you specifically last night and this morning, and he will think about you so many times today you can't even count them.

When you are confronted by temptation, consider praying the prayer David prayed at the end of Psalm 139:

> **Search me, O God, and know my heart;**
>
> **test me and know my anxious thoughts.**
>
> **Point out anything in me that offends you,**
>
> **and lead me along the path of everlasting life.**
>
> PSALM 139:23-24, NLT

CHAPTER 9

Addictions Aren't Funny

So Avoid Them at All Costs

I love a drink, but I never encouraged drunkenness
by harping on its alleged funny side.

MARK TWAIN, *ABROAD WITH MARK TWAIN AND EUGENE FIELD*

✦

Do something every day that you don't want to do; this is the golden
rule for acquiring the habit of doing your duty without pain.

MARK TWAIN, *FOLLOWING THE EQUATOR*

DO YOU EVER WATCH television reruns from the ancient past? *Hee Haw* was a country music show whose cast performed skits portraying hillbillies. One of *Hee Haw's* regular characters was a drunk man who staggered around making the crowd laugh with his outrageous antics.

Another popular show of that era, *The Andy Griffith Show*, also featured a town drunk. Otis was portrayed as a sweet, harmless buffoon who spent most of his day snockered.

Today's television shows and movies don't portray alcoholics as lovable, funny caricatures, because that isn't realistic. Most Americans now realize that addiction is a serious, growing problem that affects millions of lives in our country. The problem encompasses much more than alcohol, with numerous addictions running rampant today.

▶ *Todd Clements*

This is a very personal subject to me. I love to have a good
time as much as anybody, but personally and professionally

I've seen the heartbreaking pain addictions bring to both the guilty and innocent.

I've seen family members spend all their money on addictions. Some of my own family members have spent time in prison because of addictions. One of my favorite cousins, who lived next door to me when I was growing up and took me fishing and hunting, died in his thirties because of alcoholism. Thinking of that cousin still bothers me today. He had so much life remaining, and he left behind two beautiful daughters and a great wife—for beer. My great-uncle committed suicide while he was drunk. Our family still misses him greatly.

An addict spreads pain and heartache not only to himself but to family and friends as well.

On a personal level I had my own problem with addictions. I had both the smarts and the willpower to beat them, but they still whipped me good in the process. It's hard to believe that something like that could have such a grip on me. From the day I got free of my addiction, I set out to learn how these things are able to trap both our minds and bodies. I never wanted to be in that situation again.

As psychiatrists we have seen plenty of hurting addicts, but we are even more upset by the countless innocent people we've known who've been hurt by addicts: children whose parents have divorced, families who are dealing with an addicted family member, parents who have lost a child to an addiction, others who have lost a loved one to a drunk driver—the list goes on and on.

Most people know very little about how addictions actually work, and some refuse to admit they have a problem even when there is ample evidence otherwise. But as professionals, we know that the best way to defeat an enemy or opponent is to know as much about the other side as possible. Governments, for example, spend billions of dollars to spy on other countries in case war breaks out and they need information. An addiction should be seen as an enemy—one that robs people of friends, family, money, and happiness in life—and the best way to defeat the threat of any addiction is to know exactly what you are dealing with.

In this chapter, we'll use the term *addictions* to refer to any kind of addiction (alcohol, drugs, gambling, pornography, food, sex, etc.). While you may never have been addicted, you most likely know an addict or have had your life touched by some form of addiction. Studies show that:

> up to half of all fatal traffic accidents involve drug use
> up to 65 percent of those who commit suicide are under the influence of drugs
> half of all murders involve alcohol
> half of the more than three hundred rapes that occur every day in this country involve alcohol
> thousands of babies are born addicted to crack each year, and thousands more are born with fetal alcohol syndrome, which often causes brain damage

Addictions also cause thousands of senseless premature deaths each year from overdoses and health problems triggered by addictions. We could write an entire book on the negative impact of addictions, but that's not our purpose in this chapter. Instead, we want to talk about the ways that addictions fool our bodies and our minds. Hardly anyone plans to become an addict. We don't know of anyone who ever said, "I want to become an alcoholic and spend much of my life in rehab." No, addictions are much more sneaky than that.

Moral versus Medical

To begin to understand the enemy, let's look at the two predominant ways in which people view addictions. We'll call them the moral model and the medical model.

Religious organizations and people who abstain from all drug and alcohol use often view addictions according to the moral model. They believe that an addiction is a weakness or a sin and also is a willful choice: a person is an alcoholic because he chooses to drink. A gambling addict enjoys her gambling and therefore willfully chooses not to give it up, even though she has lost her house, job, and family. The inability to stop the addiction is seen as a weakness in moral character among people who have little or no willpower.

Proponents of the moral model might tell an addict, "If you had enough faith in God, you would stop using drugs." Counselors using this model often utilize guilt as a tool to drive the addict toward rehabilitation. Sadly, this is not always successful.

The medical model sees an addiction as a genetic problem that should be treated as other medical illnesses. Proponents of this perspective claim that addicts can't just quit, as subscribers to the moral model believe. Instead, because addictions are considered to be chronic, the goal is to control them.

The medical model suggests that alcoholics have inherited a gene for alcoholism, and they will always be alcoholics. Even if someone has been clean for fifty years, the medical model says that person is still an alcoholic. But in the same way that high blood pressure can be controlled through diet, exercise, and medicine, alcoholism can be controlled with lifelong treatment.

Many drug treatment programs are based on the medical model. Their goal is not to help people overcome drug use, but rather help them reach an acceptable level of use that interferes minimally with daily life.

The medical model takes away a person's power to deal with his or her own life. It also says a person is always an addict, even if that person stops his or her habit. That doesn't make sense; a person cannot be addicted if he or she doesn't partake in that habit.

Which Model Is Right?

While elements of both models have greatly helped millions of addicts, neither one is completely right. The truth lies somewhere in the middle.

Most of the alcoholics we treat don't really know why they are so driven to drink. They only know that in spite of their best attempts to quit, they can't seem to do it on their own. Addicts don't enjoy being addicted, and they would desperately like to be free. But neither the moral model nor the medical model adequately addresses the problem in its entirety.

It's important to understand that two things drive all addictions: shame and lack of connectedness.

Of course, everyone feels ashamed from time to time. True shame should be taken to God for forgiveness. But shame often stems from false guilt. A child who is criticized a lot growing up or is physically, verbally, or sexually abused blames herself for being the victim of abuse. She feels shame, even into adulthood, when there is no logical reason to feel ashamed. The abuser is the guilty one, not the victim of abuse. The shame that drives most addictions is of this false guilt variety.

Sometimes we are ashamed of having normal feelings, so we deny or ignore them, pretending they are not there. For example, many people have been taught that it's sinful to be angry (in spite of what the Bible says in Ephesians 4:26), so when they feel anger, they either lie to themselves by denying it, or feel ashamed and guilty for what is actually a very normal emotion.

Addictions—to alcohol, drugs, pornography, and other things—numb the pain of these repressed emotions. The cure for addictions, therefore, is never just simply abstaining from the substances or behaviors. The cure is found in relieving the false guilt through wise counsel and spiritual growth, and then getting connected, possibly to a prayer partner, a spouse, a best friend, or a recovery group. Being connected with friends or family members who love us in spite of our faults and allow us to be honest about our feelings helps to eliminate the shame and loneliness that drives us toward addiction.

When people with addictions come to our day program, we start treatment by giving them nonaddictive medication to help minimize cravings and avoid painful withdrawal. Then our counselors perform psychiatric testing to help clients get to the root of their problems. Once we have a better handle on the cause of the addictions, we help the patients get in touch with repressed emotions and find relief from them. Often, once patients have relieved their shame and gotten connected to the other patients in group therapy, they find little or no desire to return to the addictions. If the root problems are not resolved, however, the clients may experience so much physical and psychological distress that they return to the addiction.

People can and do have the power to overcome addictions. Willpower works, but where it works best is in helping us avoid addictions in the first place. The more you understand about how addictions work, the better prepared you are to beat them. Let's take a scientific look at how addictions start, develop, and eventually control people's lives.

How Do Addictions Start?

Addictive drugs or behaviors give a pleasing sensation to the body. Downers like alcohol, marijuana, and narcotics (pain pills, heroin, and opiates) relax the body and create a sense of euphoria. Uppers, such as cocaine, provide a burst of energy, increase self-confidence, and create a sense of well-being. For some people, gambling and pornography act as downers, while for others, these addictions act as uppers. Food addictions create a relaxing sense of well-being. The person enjoys the feeling associated with these substances or activities and, therefore, wants to continue to use them.

Some people learn after time to use an upper when they are feeling down and a downer when they are tense or uptight. People use alcohol to calm down when they are in situations that make them nervous, such as parties or blind dates. Uppers are often used to help regain self-confidence or work long hours in a job.

More than 250 million prescriptions are written in America each year for downers, which means that a lot of people are just floating through existence.[5] Unfortunately, people on downers still end up feeling the pain they are trying to avoid, because after a while, the body becomes immune to the high these drugs give.

Some of these substances do have medicinal value. Opiates, marijuana, and cocaine can all relieve pain. Alcohol, marijuana, and medicines like Xanax work well for anxiety. Amphetamines help many people concentrate and be more productive, gain self-confidence, and lose weight. The problem with using these illegally or outside a doctor's care, however, is that the risks far outweigh the benefits.

How Do Addictions Develop?

The reward centers in our brains are very powerful. During some scientific experiments, mice were locked in a cage and could push a lever and receive a small amount of cocaine. This was pleasurable for the mice, and they pushed the lever over and over. Later the doors to the cage were opened and food was placed outside the cage. The mice had the freedom to leave—and to eat—but they chose instead to stay in the cage and push that bar over and over, some even to the point of death by starvation or exhaustion.

We've all heard the phrase "hooked on drugs." Just what does that mean? John Prather, a mild-mannered and shy sixteen-year-old, found out.

▶ *Todd Clements*

Homecoming always filled John with dread. Although he enjoyed the football game, just thinking about the homecoming dance after the game made him nervous. John hated asking girls to dance because he was overweight and felt awkward on the dance floor. He usually sat back with a group of guys and watched the action from the bleachers.

But this year was different. About thirty minutes before the dance started, Sam persuaded John to try a white powdery pill. John noticed an almost instant wave of energy come over him, along with a surge of self-esteem and courage. John initiated conversations with classmates he had never spoken to before, and he danced with several girls he normally would have been too nervous to approach. As he did so, he realized that his dancing was better than most of the other guys' in the room. When the music ended and the lights came on at 1 a.m., John was still wide awake and couldn't believe the dance was over.

John enjoyed the feeling of self-confidence he experienced that night, especially around females. He could hardly believe it when Sam told him that in addition to providing energy, the white pill could also help him lose weight. Sam had enough for one more dose each, which the two boys swallowed before school on Monday morning. John felt good all morning, listening like never before in class. When lunchtime came he was not even hungry. He did notice a headache and tiredness that afternoon but thought little about it. He was sure that if he could get some more of that drug, he could earn better grades, lose weight, and even make more friends—perhaps even find a girlfriend.

Sam said he knew a guy they could buy more pills from. John used the money from his part-time job at the supermarket and began to take one each morning before school. His grades did improve, and he lost ten pounds, but the pills always wore off by the end of the school day, leaving John

with little energy to sack groceries at the supermarket. Taking
a second pill around three in the afternoon took care of that
problem. His energy level at work was so high he could
unload crates of fifty-pound dog food bags without a break.
The boss appreciated John's new enthusiasm.

The headaches and irritability returned at night when he got
home, leaving John with little patience for his family. If something didn't go his way he became easily angered and lost his
temper. He also wasn't sleeping very well. In the mornings he
felt dead tired, at least until he had taken his pill. After several
weeks John had to add a third pill, which meant he had to
work more hours at the store and even weekends to earn more
money. Although his grades initially improved, they fell again
because he had less time to study. After work his mind was
so tired he could hardly think, and his body felt so agitated he
could hardly sit still. Sam gave him some pills to take for the
agitation, and he found that these new pills also helped him
sleep. They worked great, but they also cost John more money.

When John's pills wore off, he could hardly stand to be
around people. He argued with his parents and his teachers,
and was almost fired for being rude to a customer. John worried constantly about getting caught with drugs. His store had
a policy of random drug testing, and he knew if he were ever
chosen, that would be the end of his job.

When the amphetamine wore off, John felt absolutely horrible, and he now had to take two pills at a time to feel better.
He realized that in the beginning he took the pills for the surge
of energy and confidence but now had to take them in order to
quit feeling bad. Eventually he was taking several pills during
the day just to feel normal and another pill at night to sleep.

The whole routine made no sense, and John finally decided to quit taking all the pills. But after only one night without them, he felt so terrible he knew he couldn't make it through the day. So he started again.

Sam introduced John to a new drug that would help calm the low periods during the day between drug doses. This one had to be injected. But it calmed him enormously—even though it sometimes nauseated him. He also had to take laxatives because the new medicine caused constipation, and he had to wear long-sleeved shirts so people wouldn't notice the needle marks in his arms.

He always carried medicine with him in case the nausea got too bad. Now John was taking a pill to get up, pills during the day to feel normal, pills to sleep, and pills to go to the bathroom. He took shots to calm himself until it was time for the next pill, dealt with daily nausea, and wore long-sleeved shirts even when it was hot. Something had to give, and it soon did!

John's supplier was arrested and thrown into jail. Without any of his pills John soon began to suffer horrible withdrawal symptoms. He began vomiting and shaking uncontrollably, and his parents took him to the hospital. There, John finally confessed what he had been doing. He was admitted into an inpatient detoxification unit, and that's where he began therapy.

Alcohol

Of every ten people that start drinking, one becomes an alcoholic. Why is it that nine can take it or leave it but one can't put it down? Is that person weak in willpower? Or does that person have a gene the others don't have? To answer this question, let's look at alcohol in depth.

Alcohol affects people in different ways. Some people drink alcohol to help them calm down and relax enough to sleep. Others may drink to relieve anxiety around a crowd. Alcohol helps introverted people become more extroverted. Alcohol gives some people a boost of self-esteem, while it makes others mean or sleepy or dizzy. Alcohol increases sexual desire in both males and females. Alcohol affects the part of the brain that inhibits emotions, so it makes it easier for a person to express his or her feelings.

At higher levels, alcohol interferes with thinking, reflexes, coordination, and balance. As the level of alcohol continues to increase, the body sees it as a toxin and starts trying to get rid of it. The person becomes nauseated and vomits. At even higher levels the person passes out. Finally, coma or death result.

Chronic heavy usage of alcohol leads to health problems, most notably ulcers, brain damage, and liver damage. Heavy drinkers usually die many years younger than the general population.

Alcohol affects each person's brain differently. People who get the most pleasurable feelings from alcohol also have the strongest cravings and are at the highest risk. Intense craving and constant thinking about a drug is considered to be a psychological addiction. But alcohol also hooks people by physical addiction as well.

Anyone who has ever drunk heavily has probably suffered from a hangover the next day. Hangovers consist of headaches, nausea, thirst, low energy and motivation, sensitivity to noise and light, and an overall feeling of depression. Only two things will get rid of a hangover: time or more alcohol. Many people start drinking again because the hangover is so miserable. This is when they get hooked.

As time progresses and they become more alcohol dependent, they find that they become very sick if they go without a drink for too long. Therefore, they *have* to drink alcohol just to feel normal. Stopping abruptly can be life threatening, as alcoholics can go into seizures and die within as little as twenty-four to forty-eight hours without a drink. Alcoholics in withdrawal also experience an extremely uncomfortable condition called delirium tremens (DTs) in which the death rate is around

20 percent. That is why serious alcoholics have to be admitted into a hospital to undergo the detoxification process. Here they can be given medicine to prevent seizures and DTs.

Alcoholics can and do recover from addiction. Alcoholics Anonymous has helped millions of people recover. Studies show that those who are most successful in Alcoholics Anonymous have good sponsors to hold them accountable.

Many people look at drinking alcohol as a moral choice. The Bible references alcohol more than one hundred times, sometimes positively and sometimes negatively. But it's very clear in its warnings against using strong drinks and getting drunk.

Few alcoholics live an enjoyable life. Most of them waste their lives and talents living for the next drink. We always recommend totally abstaining from alcohol to anyone who has been an alcoholic. Please, don't waste your life.

Marijuana

Marijuana (also known as cannabis or pot) has been in the news a lot recently because proponents want to legalize it for medicinal purposes, mainly as a painkiller and to relieve nausea in cancer patients undergoing chemotherapy. Marijuana is illegal in the United States, but an estimated 5 percent of the population uses it on a monthly basis. Marijuana comes from several different types of plants grown all around the world, and it is ingested by smoking or eating the dried plant. Its active ingredient is THC. Most of the marijuana in America comes from Mexico and South America, and today's crops are about five times as potent as the marijuana grown in the 1960s.

Marijuana releases the neurotransmitter anandamide. The physical effects include relaxation or sedation, pain control, an increase in appetite, bloodshot eyes, coughing from lung irritation, and a loss in muscular coordination. Usually people feel aloof and have trouble concentrating. Marijuana disrupts short-term memory and distorts a person's sense of time. Most people report the overall effects to be pleasurable, but some people do experience unpleasant feelings of paranoia and even hallucinations.

Proponents of marijuana claim it is not addicting and doesn't create health problems, but that is not exactly true. Studies do show that the drug is psychologically addicting—the user craves the drug and builds up a tolerance to it, which means he or she continually has to smoke more in order to achieve the same effects. Those who stop smoking it also experience withdrawal symptoms such as anger, irritability, and severe depression. Counselors note that with the newer forms of more potent marijuana, beginning users sometimes experience acute anxiety and psychotic reactions that cause them to lose control of their mental state. During these "bad trips," a marijuana user is at high risk for dangerous or harmful activities. There have been some reports of teens not coming down off this state and remaining in a continual state of confusion. Marijuana use impairs driving ability and also causes brain damage. [6]

As psychiatrists, we have studied brain scans of people who have smoked pot once a day or more for several years, and seen holes in the brain where cells have died or become dysfunctional. This brain damage remains even when the patient quits smoking pot. Marijuana is also often the gateway drug to heavier drug use.

In other words, smoking pot is a really stupid thing to do. If you say it helps you come out of your shell and socialize with ease because you inherited social phobia, we will say, "Great, but wouldn't you rather get into treatment and work on the root causes of your anxiety?"

If you say, "Pot makes me feel okay about myself for a while, even though I am participating in all sorts of sin," then we would say, "What are the reasons you are so tempted to commit those particular sins? Are you lonely? Do you feel unloved? Do you feel unforgivable? Do you feel powerless? Do you have severe inferiority feelings? Why not get Christian counseling to learn how to meet all those needs spiritually and emotionally, without medications or illegal drugs?"

Many of the marijuana users we have met in our practices are depressed people who use the drug to numb their feelings. But this never resolves anything. In fact it makes depression worse, and the suicide rate is actually higher for pot smokers, who are usually very lonely people. Who wants to live her one and only life in a continual fog? Yes, it may numb you from feeling painful emotions, but it also numbs you from feeling happy emotions. Marijuana also causes an amotivational syndrome, which means those who use it for a long time have no motivation to do anything with their lives except sit on the couch.

Opioids

The opioids category contains several drugs, such as heroin and morphine and other legal painkillers. Although heroin is illegal, the other substances are used in medicine to treat acute pain, coughs, and diarrhea. Opioids can be taken by mouth, smoked, snorted, or used intravenously. People use them for nonmedical reasons to drown out emotional pain, get a rush of euphoria, and block the withdrawal effects of other drugs. Opioids are extremely addicting. They hit the brain's reward pathway very strongly. They also build a quick tolerance, which means the user has to keep increasing the dose. People using the medicine for pain control usually only become addicts when they keep using the drug past the point of pain relief.

Opioids also cause itching and nausea, lower sexual desire, and interfere with women's hormones. The physical withdrawal symptoms include painful stomach cramps, continuous diarrhea, vomiting, allover muscle pain, an inability to sleep, and fever. Many people suffering from withdrawal feel as if they are going to die. Some wish they could die, just to escape their misery. And some do die.

Psychologically, opiate addicts report intense cravings for the drugs, even years after they stop taking them. Once addicted, a person generally struggles for the rest of her life. Fortunately, various medications are available that are safe and nonaddictive and can help reduce opioid cravings for those who seek treatment.

Heroin is the most dangerous of the opioids. It produces a quick rush of extreme euphoria but only lasts a few minutes. Addicts can spend hundreds of dollars a day just to get their fix of heroin. Many people have died from overdosing on this drug.

Most heroin users inject the drug with needles, so there is also a high incidence of HIV infection among heroin addicts. Many people also use heroin along with an amphetamine. This is called speedballing, which is very dangerous because of the high potential for death in an overdose. Again, medication is available to help a recovering heroin addict deal with cravings.

Sedatives

Sedatives are downers that include drugs like Xanax, Valium, and Ativan. These drugs are legal and are used mostly to decrease anxiety and stop panic attacks. They are similar to alcohol in the way they work, calming restlessness and inducing sleep. When these medicines first came out in the 1960s, they were hailed as nonaddictive miracle drugs. However, we have since realized they can be very addicting.

After only a few months of continual use of one of these drugs, people trying to stop will experience symptoms of withdrawal. Withdrawal causes extreme anxiety, an inability to sleep, severe depression, and seizures. Longtime users report lifelong cravings for the drugs, which can be deadly in an overdose, especially if mixed with alcohol.

Rohypnol, another sedative, has been called the date-rape drug because it can easily be slipped into a drink, causing a person to pass out. GHB, another drug in this class, is used frequently among teens for its euphoric rush. These drugs are often bought off the street from "street chemists," so it's difficult to know exactly what's in them.

Cocaine and amphetamines (speed)

These uppers give a surge of energy, increased confidence, motivation, and a feeling of well-being. Unfortunately, they only offer borrowed energy, which must be paid for later. Many people who are depressed use these drugs to feel better about themselves, but in the end they find that their situations are worse. These drugs affect the brain's distribution of norepinephrine and epinephrine, which are forms of adrenaline and very important in regulating moods. People who are depressed usually have low amounts of these chemicals, which results in sadness, low energy levels, and an inability to concentrate. Cocaine use causes the brain to shoot out large amounts of both these chemicals, which creates a temporary sense of euphoria. However, repeated drug use actually depletes the brain's supply, resulting in depression.

Stimulants also affect another brain chemical, dopamine. By triggering a dopamine release, these drugs fool your brain into thinking that hunger has been satisfied when no food has been eaten and that sexual desire has been satisfied when no sexual activity has occurred. This stimulation also brings with it an overall rush of well-being and pleasure. As the drug is used more and more, however, the rush diminishes and what is known as "crashing" begins to occur.

Crashing occurs after the effects of the drug wear off. When crashing, people have no energy, and then they are too uncomfortable to sleep. When sleep does happen, it is usually accompanied by nightmares. Users also report depression and an intense craving for the drug. Many suicides take place when a drug user is crashing.

Since dopamine is one of the chemicals God created to keep us functioning normally, interfering with it through illegal drugs can actually drive a person insane, producing delusions of grandeur or paranoia. Long-term use of stimulants can permanently affect the brain's ability to produce these neurochemicals. And when the brain stops producing the necessary chemicals, the user has to rely on artificial stimulants just to keep dopamine and norepinephrine levels normal.

Over three thousand deaths occur in this country every year due to cocaine overdose. A dose that causes no problems one day might precipitate a heart attack the next day. Cocaine has also been reported to cause strokes.[7]

Amphetamines have much the same affect as cocaine, but they are more widespread because they are cheaper and easier to make. Amphetamine use is a growing problem among teens in our country. There are more than three hundred ways to manufacture amphetamines, also known as "crank" and "crystal," and much of this is made in home laboratories, which is very dangerous in itself. A defining characteristic of amphetamine users is a mouth full of rotten teeth.

We have both seen teens affected by *amphetamine psychosis*, which is paranoia, increased suspiciousness, and misinterpretation of others' actions, which often leads to violence. I (Dr. Clements) had a patient who beheaded both of his parents when he was nineteen years old. He was a bright young man when I knew him, but because of his addiction, he'll spend the rest of his life behind bars.

Amphetamines do have some legitimate medical uses, especially as treatment for attention-deficit/hyperactivity disorder (ADHD), traumatic brain injury, and chronic fatigue syndrome.

Even caffeine could be considered a stimulant, albeit much weaker than amphetamines. Eighty-five percent of the American population consumes substantial amounts of caffeine. Caffeine is known to be safe in moderation, but too much can make people nervous and panicky and can cause headaches.

Nicotine, another stimulant, is quite addictive because it both stimulates and calms. There is enough in the news already about the dangers of smoking, so we will say only this: Anyone who wants to quit smoking can do so by using a nonaddictive medication, which can be prescribed by a doctor.

Pornography

Earlier we alluded to the fact that one out of every ten people who start drinking alcohol will become an alcoholic, a capture rate of 10 percent. Of all the addictions, pornography has the highest capture rate: 90 percent.[8] That's right; nine out of every ten adolescent males who start viewing pornography will become addicted. Why? Pornography's effect on the brain is almost identical to the effect caused by a stimulant.

When someone views pornography, his brain releases dopamine and norepinephrine, causing a powerful rush of excitement and euphoria. That is why the pornography business last year made more money than the NFL, NBA, NHL, and MLB all put together.[9]

The Internet has made pornography more accessible than ever before. In the past, a person had to go to an adult store to buy a magazine or a movie. Today, people can sit at work and watch pornography on their computers. In the same way that the brain becomes tolerant to drugs, viewing pornography after a while gives less and less of a rush.

Porn addicts then move on to acting out fantasies in order to get the same feeling of euphoria. They do this by going to strip clubs or hiring prostitutes. Rapists nearly always trace their crime back to a pornography addiction. Married addicts usually report trouble in their marriages, especially in the area of sexuality. Pornography addictions have ruined thousands of good marriages, careers, and reputations, not to mention having horrible effects on the young men and women who pose for magazines or videos. Porn teaches society to view women as merely objects to be used, rather than the valuable daughters of God with eternal souls that they are.

Gambling

The United States has recently seen a resurgence of gambling addictions. In the past, big-time gamblers had to travel to Las Vegas in order to feed their addictions. Today, however, gambling riverboats can be found on almost every creek in the country. The Internet also offers plenty of gambling on sporting events, and televised poker tournaments have made this card came popular again.

One client—a Native American casino manager in Oklahoma—said he had to enlarge his poker rooms in recent years. These rooms used to be filled with old men and cigar smoke. Today they are packed with young men and women. Apparently the old men are making money by cleaning out the wallets of the younger generation.

Food

Food is a very common addiction in this country. We are a country where two out of three people are overweight, and one out of five is downright obese.[10] We're eating ourselves to death, and binge eating is becoming all too common. Large servings of food affect people much like downers do. Carbohydrates, especially, convey a soothing sense of calm because they release serotonin, a chemical the brain uses to relax us and help us sleep.

Reports show that food addiction is highest among lonely people.[11] Cravings often occur late at night while a person is alone, usually watching TV. Shame and lack of connectedness are the root causes of most eating addictions, just like any other addiction.

Weight gain is also a method of avoiding intimacy. Some people consciously or unconsciously eat to gain weight in order to keep the other sex from being attracted to them. This is generally based on childhood sexual molestation, after which intimacy becomes coupled with sex in a person's mind, and the thought is repulsive.

Food addictions are often harder to break than other addictions. People can do without drugs, gambling, or pornography, but they cannot live without food, so they are continually exposed to it. Alcoholics, with proper treatment, can quit drinking altogether, but food addicts can never quit eating. Nearly all eating addictions have a root cause, so we always recommend a thorough psychological evaluation. We never recommend diets—only lifestyle changes.

A young lady was a normal weight all her life until she was raped at age seventeen. Then she ballooned up to three hundred pounds. Although she didn't realize it, she had gained weight in order to keep such a thing from happening again. She could lose all that weight on a diet, but if she did it without resolving her fears, she would simply regain the weight and not know why.

Thirty-five out of thirty-six people who lose weight by dieting regain it within one year. Resolving root problems is the best way to ensure permanent weight loss or restore healthy eating patterns for those with other eating disorders such as bulimia and anorexia.

The Bottom Line

In truth, almost anything can become an addiction—working out, playing golf, hunting, watching TV, sewing, reading, even going to church. It would take a huge book to address every addiction.

We are beginning to learn more and more about the science of addiction and what goes on in the brain. Modern science would like to blame it on genetics, and there *are* some genetic components, but the bottom line is that social factors play a huge role in addictions. Many people use addictions to fit in with a crowd or escape unwanted feelings, especially loneliness and shame. The only way to truly escape these feelings is to deal with them and make whatever changes in your life are necessary.

Consider what you can do to get rid of your shame and to connect with other people on a gut level. So many young people with magnetic personalities, brilliant minds, and caring hearts have ruined their lives because of addictions. Don't add yourself to that list. If you have or do develop an addiction, be courageous enough to get help.

Good treatment and support is available, but help won't come looking for you. You will have to take the first step.

CHAPTER 10

Happiness Is Doing What You Love

So Love What You Do

The thing for us to do is just to do our duty and not worry about whether anybody sees us or not.

MARK TWAIN, *THE ADVENTURES OF HUCKLEBERRY FINN*

COUNTRY SINGER JOHNNY PAYCHECK released the number one hit "Take This Job and Shove It" in the 1970s. The song featured a man who hated everything about his job, including the boss. One day he finally reached the breaking point and told his boss in a graphic way that he was finished working there.

Over the years, this has become something of a theme song for those who are unhappy in their jobs. Statistics show that a good number of Americans wish they had a different job. In our practices, we often see people who are unhappy in their jobs, and this discontent usually leads to an overall feeling of unhappiness in life as well. If you remember nothing else from this chapter, remember this next statement: It is almost impossible to be happy if you don't like your job or your marriage. Fortunately, with God, all things are possible.

We've already talked about the poor choices that lead people into a bad marriage. But in this chapter we'll focus on the importance of finding and keeping the right job. Think about it. There are 168 hours in a week. The average person spends one third of those hours working (including time spent getting ready for work and commuting). Another third is spent getting ready for bed and sleeping, leaving only a third of a person's week for everything else: family obligations, ministries, home maintenance, hobbies, etc. It is easy to see why unhappiness on the job has such a profound effect.

So many people we see in our practices tell us, "If I knew then what I know now, my life would be much happier." This statement has driven us to find out exactly what these people now know. We hope by sharing those insights with you we can help you to avoid that unhappy place our clients find themselves in. Major decisions affect your life in every way every day. Don't take them lightly.

People can and do change jobs every day in America. That is one of the great things about living in a free country. Some people change companies but stay in the same vocation, which usually requires only minor readjustments. Others, however, totally change careers, which requires major life changes. As our society becomes more technical and specialized, it has become more difficult and time consuming to make midlife career changes. But how are we expected to know in our teens and twenties what we want to do day in, day out for the rest of our lives? Here are a few ideas that should help.

Get a Good Education

My (Dr. Clements) grandfather was a lawyer and judge who had many wise sayings, including this one: "Education is the only thing that people pay for and don't care whether they get or not." How many people do you know who paid thousands of dollars for college and then skipped classes?

During my (Dr. Clements) first year of college, I knew plenty of kids who stayed up all night playing Nintendo and then slept in until noon. And although they (or their parents) had paid thousands of dollars in tuition, many of them never returned to school after Christmas break. These same people who laugh about flunking all their classes would never dream of paying that much money for a car that didn't work.

▶ *Todd Clements*

A friend of mine is a college professor who has a reputation for being so tough that students try to avoid his classes. As a young professor, he had given the first test of the semester several weeks into the course of a particular class. Much to his surprise, half the class flunked the test. These grades upset him, as he did not want to fail anyone, so he decided he would let students retake the test. But handing out the dreaded test scores brought the biggest surprise of his life.

Rather than being upset, many of the students who failed the test were laughing, pointing to their tests, and showing others their flunking score. What he thought would cause weeping and gnashing of teeth was only a big joke in the eyes of his students.

My friend decided right then and there that if the students didn't care, he wasn't going to care either. Rather than making an appointment to discuss the test with him, most of the students who failed simply went to the registrar's office and dropped the class. The drop-class form asked students to give a reason for canceling the class, and the most common reason given was that the subject matter was irrelevant.

Today this professor still administers a difficult first test. Many students still laughingly parade their failing score around the room and then drop the class the next day. But for the rest of the semester, he knows that the small nucleus of students who remain are ready to study and learn.

Why is education so important, especially when much of it seems irrelevant? Listen to any politician running for election and you'll probably hear these three words: the American dream. The American dream is the expectation that anyone can become something in America, regardless of socioeconomic status.

I (Dr. Meier) am living proof of the American dream. My parents were both German immigrants. My mom never learned to drive. As I've already mentioned, my dad was a carpenter, and I had planned on being a carpenter too. But after the dreams I had at sixteen, I changed all my courses, studied harder, got better grades, and became a physician. Then I specialized in psychiatry and got a seminary degree. I love America.

This may not sound so amazing if you have been raised in the United States, but for some, it is nearly incomprehensible. In caste societies, you are born into a socioeconomic group and can never move from that group. If your parents are peasants, you will also live as a peasant, no matter how smart or talented you are. Your standing in society depends on the family you are born into.

While it is true that the wealthy have more advantages in our country, anyone can move up or down the ladder. However, there is one secret that makes such mobility much easier: education.

Several organizations from our community hosted receptions for my (Dr. Clements) high school senior class the week of graduation. During one of these parties, I asked one of my classmates if he planned to go to college. His reply was hostile: "College? I've got a job at [the local factory] making $6.50 an hour. I've been in this prison [school] for twelve years already! Why would I want to go to college?"

All I could say was, "Yeah, I see what you mean." He's probably up to $10 an hour today.

I see many young people in my work just like this who have no idea about the value of an education. They give me all kinds of excuses as to why they don't want to further their education. They range from "I'm burned out on studying" to "The stuff you learn is useless." But is taking a break from studying worth working a McJob the rest of their lives? (Yes, *McJob* is a word in the current [eleventh] edition of *Merriam-Webster's*

Collegiate Dictionary. It is a "low-paying job that requires little skill and provides little opportunity for advancement.")

Education does not guarantee success, and neither does a lack of education guarantee failure. Millions of people without a higher education have become successful. But in this day and culture, education does provide a person with an important advantage. In the days of our grandparents, a high school or college degree was not needed in the way it is today. Many jobs were learned through the apprentice system, where a person got on-the-job training from someone skilled in a specific type of work. Today on-the-job training still exists, but many companies require a college degree, or at the very least a high school diploma, no matter what skills the job entails.

A college diploma demonstrates to a prospective employer that the graduate is responsible and teachable. An education also allows a person to have more control in choosing his or her career path.

We've talked to many successful people who don't have a formal education. And most of them still say they would have liked to have gone to college or graduated from high school. Though college degrees can be quite expensive, numerous scholarships and no- or low-interest loans are available to those who want to go to school. Sometimes, a student might have to work a daytime job and take night courses until he or she earns an undergraduate or master's degree. With determination, there is always a way to achieve that goal.

Choose Satisfaction over Salary

▶ *Todd Clements*

Every year, U.S. News and World Report *publishes the average incomes of physicians, graphing and comparing the salaries for each medical specialty. The administration at my medical school passed these out to the medical students while I was still attending (I think it was to give us hope, since most of us were barely getting by, living off student loans). Interestingly, some of my classmates used these reports to decide what specialty of medicine to pursue.*

One of my friends abruptly changed his plans during his third year, switching his goal from being an emergency room doctor to becoming a surgeon. When I asked him why he made the change, he said that although he loved the excitement and fast pace of the emergency room, surgeons could make $300,000 per year. Most ER physicians at the time only earned around $200,000.

My friend hadn't even taken into account the fact that surgeons work more hours, spend more years training, and have higher malpractice insurance rates than ER doctors. The kicker was when he admitted that he really didn't like surgery, but he hoped it would grow on him.

I've got some startling news for my old friend—the guy who earns $200,000 is just as happy as the guy who earns $300,000. What difference would it make in your life if you made $300,000 as opposed to $200,000? You could buy some more stuff. But guess what? Stuff will not make you happy.

Do you want to know what happened to my friend? He entered a demanding surgical field. A few years ago his wife divorced him because he was never home. Today, after paying alimony and child support, his annual income is significantly less than $200,000.

We ran into each other a few months ago, and he claims he likes his career. However, he's currently working hard to save enough money so he can retire in his fifties.

Are we saying you shouldn't consider money in your career decisions? By no means! But money should definitely not be the only consideration. If you are miserable in a job, no amount of money will make it enjoyable. Who wants to live a life like that?

When I (Dr. Meier) finished my psychiatry residency at Duke University in 1975, I had narrowed down my job choices to three: a job in Maine for $100,000 a year, a job in Chicago for $150,000 a year, and a teaching job at Trinity Seminary for $14,000 a year.

Although I had a lot of student loan debt at the time, my wife and I both agreed that I would benefit mankind the most by teaching future pastors how to provide excellent counseling. We accepted the position at Trinity Seminary, just outside Chicago. Eighteen months later, we moved to Dallas to teach at Dallas Theological Seminary full-time for only $12,600 a year. We did what we thought God was calling us to do, regardless of pay. It wasn't without some personal struggle, however. It really hurt to turn down the big bucks after growing up poor. But many of the students I taught in those first couple of years have gone on to shake up the world for Christ in amazing ways. I know now it was one of the best decisions I ever made.

There is another extreme on this moneymaking scale as well. Ralph was one of the most interesting people I (Dr. Clements) had ever met. He loved to play cards and knew about every card game imaginable. The problem was he tried to make a career of that. He spent most of his evenings playing poker in back rooms of Oklahoma casinos. When he wasn't playing, he was out trying to rustle up people to take card lessons. He barely scraped by. His family and friends all told him to go to college, but he refused.

I tried to help Ralph realize that when he married and had kids, he wouldn't want to spend every night in a smoky casino. Also, relying on poker winnings to live and raise a family is not a secure life. Last I heard Ralph had moved to Las Vegas.

Look into the Future

I (Dr. Clements) spent my college summers as a camp counselor. I loved that job and made a lot of friends. I dreamed of making it my career. Then it hit me—*I can't be a camp counselor when I am fifty*. I made a hundred dollars a week, which wouldn't cut it once I had car and house payments. I could be an administrator, but that's not what I wanted to do. I wanted to be out there swimming and playing games. Many jobs we love in our twenties would not be good careers when we are fifty. Does that mean we shouldn't do those jobs? Of course not.

Professional football is a great example. I (Dr. Meier) occasionally do Bible studies for the Dallas Cowboys and have gotten to know many of the Christian players over the years. No one that I have met expects to play in the NFL until the age of fifty. Very few even make it to forty. But that shouldn't deter them from playing while they can. My advice to them is always the same: Love what you do, but never stop preparing for the rest of your life.

I (Dr. Clements) know an all-American college baseball player who majored in accounting. The other players laughed when he brought his book bag on baseball trips. But although he knew he would probably get drafted to the pros, he also wanted to be prepared for what would come after that. He loved accounting and said, "This is what I'll be doing when I'm sixty; it will be easier to learn now than when I'm middle-aged."

His words ring so true. We're certainly not saying that you have to plan out every year of your life or know exactly what you will be doing when you are sixty. However, an old saying that hung at my summer camp rifle range warned us, "Those who aim for nothing are sure to hit their target every time." Start aiming for greatness now.

Give It Your Best

Consider the parable of the talents found in Matthew 25. This parable is about a master who gave each of his servants a different amount of money to use while he was gone. A talent was approximately one thousand dollars. To one servant he gave five talents, to another two, and to the last he gave one. The servant with five put his to work and made five more; the one with two doubled his as well. The servant with one talent did nothing except to hide it. When the master returned, he was angry with the servant who hid his money. He gave that servant's talent to the man who now had ten, and then threw the servant out of the house.

Jesus used this parable to show us that God expects us to do what we can with what we've got. Some of us have been given more "talents" than others. Some have more money, some are smarter, some are better looking. But that does not matter to God. He was just as pleased with the servant who made two talents as he was with the man who made five.

Be careful not to let the world's mind-set creep into your way of thinking. Consider the following politically correct version of the parable of the talents:

> A master who was going on a trip called together his servants and entrusted his property to them. To one he gave five talents, to one he gave two, and to another he gave one. The one with five talents at once went to work and gained five more; the one with two also did the same, adding two more talents. The servant with one hid his talent, then went and asked the other two servants if he could borrow a few of their talents. They said no.
>
> The master returned and became angry with the first two servants for not giving away their talents. He then collected the fifteen talents and evenly distributed five to each of them. The first two servants were disappointed but took their five talents and again went to make more. The last servant went to hide his new five talents like he had the first one.

The world tries to sell us the idea that money, food, education, and health care should be distributed evenly, regardless of whether or not we work. Even though communism is all but dead, this mentality lingers on. The Bible, however, says that people who are able to work but refuse should not even eat.

Have you ever wondered if there will be toilets in heaven? Who knows? The Bible says that Jesus ate after he got his new body, and we know there will be banquets in heaven. We also learn from the book of Revelation that twelve different trees in heaven will bear leaves for healing the nations of all illnesses in the New Jerusalem. Maybe God will give us bodies that simply evaporate the food, and we won't need heavenly toilets. But if there are toilets in heaven, we bet they will be sparkling clean.

Do you want to succeed? Then take whatever job you have been given and do it to the best of your ability. People don't start at the top—they rise to the top. If your job is cleaning toilets, then vow to have the cleanest toilets around. Work as if you are cleaning toilets in heaven. If you want to rise to the next level, strive to be the very best at your current level.

Consider no work to be beneath you. God doesn't expect you to do things he has not given you the ability to do, but he does expect you to give your all in whatever you've been given to do.

The Bottom Line

You'll always be frustrated if you are working to please people. To paraphrase an old saying, "You can please some of the people some of the time, but not all of the people all of the time." Nothing is as disheartening as going the extra mile to please someone and finding that your work has gone unnoticed. Work at pleasing God, because he will always notice.

> **Am I now trying to win the approval of men, or of God? Or am I trying to please men? If I were still trying to please men, I would not be a servant of Christ** GALATIANS 1:10

CHAPTER 11

God Has a Plan for Your Life

So Never Settle for Second Best

*No man that has ever lived has done a thing to please
God—primarily. It was done to please himself, then God next.*

MARK TWAIN, *MARK TWAIN, A BIOGRAPHY*

✦

*There are many scapegoats for our sins, but
the most popular one is Providence.*

MARK TWAIN, "NOTEBOOK," 1898

WHEN I WAS IN college, I (Dr. Clements) had a nine-foot pet snake named Ichabod. He served two purposes: He provided entertainment once a month for my fraternity brothers when we fed him, and my sister wore him around her neck during the bathing suit portion of a beauty contest. Needless to say, she won the swimsuit competition. The rest of the time, Ichabod basically lay in his cage, breathing air and taking up space.

Unlike Ichabod, we do not live only to eat, breathe, take up space, and provide occasional entertainment. God actually has a purpose for our lives, and when we discover that purpose, we discover God's will. God wants us to seek and find his will; he'll never force it on us. Sadly, many people—even many Christians—don't follow his will for their lives, so they miss out. For when we realize God's purpose, we have a chance to live the most meaningful life possible. If we don't, we'll only be settling for second best.

How often have you asked yourself, *What is God's will for my life?*

Does it feel as if God enjoys keeping it a secret from you? We deal with Christians every day who suffer from depression, anxiety, or fearfulness because they're struggling with these difficult life questions. Many of these patients feel as if God has deserted them in their time of need and uncertainty, especially if their earthly fathers did the same thing when they were children. When we pray, we are often subconsciously praying to a heavenly version of our earthly fathers. That can be pretty scary. At this point, some Christians give up in despair and turn to others to tell them what to do rather than waiting on the Lord. That's when they really get into trouble.

It's crucial that you find God's will for your life. Nothing else can actually take the place of knowing your purpose—not friends, family, fun, fame, or wealth. Any success apart from God's purpose is usually quite meaningless. Over the years, I (Dr. Meier) have talked to NFL players who worked all their lives to win a Super Bowl, but then when they finally did, they weren't as happy as they thought they would be. Instead, they were depressed, wondering, *Is this all there is?*

Recently a man I (Dr. Meier) knew committed suicide. He was wealthy and somewhat famous, and many people would have traded lives with this guy in a second. But his suicide note told how miserable he was and how meaningless his life had become.

King Solomon, the wisest man who ever lived, strayed from God's will and realized this same principle. He wrote the Old Testament book of Ecclesiastes, which starts out with these depressing words: "'Meaningless! Meaningless!' says the Teacher. 'Utterly meaningless! Everything is meaningless'" (Ecclesiastes 1:2).

God wants your life to be meaningful and to fulfill a purpose. Those who don't know God's purpose for their lives often try to stay busy so they don't have to think about what they are missing. But it's motion without meaning, much like Chevy Chase driving around and around Big Ben in National Lampoon's *European Vacation*. He was moving, but he wasn't going anywhere. Others try to perform as many good works as they can, hoping that will suffice, but it doesn't.

God wants us to seek out his will, and he wants it to be a joyful experience, much like an adventure. To find it, however, you must first answer two questions:

> Is Jesus your Savior? Do you believe he lived a sinless life, died on the cross for your sins, and rose again? Once you accept Jesus, you are saved from an existence of eternity without God. "God loved the people of this world so much that he gave his only Son, so that everyone who has faith in him will have eternal life and never really die" (John 3:16, CEV).

> Is Jesus the Lord of your life? Making him Lord means turning over complete control of your life to him. It is saying, *God, you have put me on this earth for a purpose, and I'm willing to serve that purpose.* There are scores of Christians who have accepted Jesus as their Savior, but not Lord; these people decide their own courses in life. Yes, they will go to heaven, but they are settling for second best on earth. To know God's will for you, you must be willing to make Jesus both Savior and Lord.

Have you taken the first step? What about the second step? Many years ago I (Dr. Meier) did a survey of my seminary students. On average, seminary students (mostly future pastors) did not make Jesus Lord of their lives until after they had been Christians for at least three years. And their characters did not begin to change until they had spent time meditating on Scripture and praying.

The Bible never says that becoming a Christian instantly gives the believer the character of Jesus. What it actually says is that "the old life is gone; a new life has begun!" (2 Corinthians 5:17, NLT). Sanctification (becoming more like Jesus) is a process. Christian therapists all over the country are helping people speed up that process.

Some Christians would rather Jesus did all the work for them, pointing to 2 Corinthians 12:9 that says God's grace is sufficient to meet all our needs. But although Christ is surely sufficient, Scripture also says that faith without works is dead (James 2:17). When your car runs out of power steering fluid, do you sit by the side of the road and wait for God to make your car run without it? No, you pray that he will help you safely walk to the nearest gas station to get more power steering fluid.

Too Close to the Fire

Some Christians spend their time seeing how close they can get to sin without being burned. These people may have Jesus as their Savior but not as their Lord. They might try to see just how far they can go sexually without actually having intercourse. Others might try to drink as much as they can without getting drunk or smoke as much pot as they can without becoming addicted. But this is like seeing how close you can drive your car to the edge of a cliff without going over. You may or may not fall over the edge, but since all your concentration is focused on not going over, you lose sight of the scenery around you, other people on the road, and even the direction of the road you are trying to follow.

This is known as playing with the devil, and the Bible warns us to do the opposite:

> **Resist the devil, and he will run from you.** JAMES 4:7, CEV

This is also known as flirting with the world. Jesus has strong words for the believer who lives this way:

> I know everything you have done, and you are not cold or hot.
> I wish you were either one or the other. But since you are luke-
> warm and neither cold nor hot, I will spit you out of my mouth.
> You claim to be rich and successful and to have everything you
> need. But you don't know how bad off you are. You are pitiful,
> poor, blind, and naked. REVELATION 3:15-17, CEV

What is it that often keeps those who have accepted Jesus as Savior from taking the second step and making him Lord? It is idolatry. We're not talking about idols like the golden calf or images of Baal. An idol is *anything* that comes between you and God.

Some idols are obvious—drugs, bad habits, bad relationships, money, power, and selfish ambition. Some idols are more subtle—your family, your friends, your job, and even your ministry. A healthy enthusiasm for these things is good, but when one of them becomes your focus in life, it becomes an idol. For many of us, the issue is control, and all of these things can be a tool for controlling our own lives.

Hebrews 11:25 says there is pleasure in sin for a season. Sometimes we would rather live off the temporary pleasure and satisfaction of sin than submit our lives to Jesus. We hate to think of anyone controlling us, even God. But if he doesn't, it won't be us that does the controlling. The devil is smart, and he will do everything he can to trick us into doing his will if God isn't in control of our lives.

Finding God's Will Is an Adventure

Finding God's will is a lot like an adventuresome road trip. Your life is the car, and you are the driver. God is riding in the front seat with you, looking at the map and navigating. The first thing many people do right before a trip is to wash and wax the outside of their cars so they look good to other people on the road. God, however, wants to clean up the inside of the car first. Romans 8:29 (NASB) says, "Those whom He foreknew, He also predestined to become conformed to the image of His Son."

The primary will of the heavenly Father for you and for me is obvious: He wants us to become more and more like his Son in our character. And since the Bible says God is love, God wants to teach us better ways to love and be loved. What could be cooler than that?

Let's say you start your trip in Dallas, Texas. God doesn't say, "Okay, we're going to Chicago." He simply says, "Go north." You have to decide whether to follow his leading or take off on your own path. God probably will not take you to Chicago in a straight line. Rather than going from Texas to Oklahoma, through Missouri, and then into Illinois, he may ask you to keep going north into Kansas first. This is where faith comes in, and you must decide whose control to follow—God's or your own.

> **With all your heart you must trust the LORD and not your own judgment. Always let him lead you, and he will clear the road for you to follow.** PROVERBS 3:5-6, CEV

As God leads you mile by mile, he'll teach you life lessons along the way. When you successfully master one mile, he'll show you the next. If he showed you the whole road at once, you'd be overwhelmed.

You must be careful because well-meaning friends and family may try to persuade you to take a shortcut. But you must be the one who decides who you will follow.

You'll want to seek out God's will for the big events in life, such as who you will marry, what career to pursue, and where you should live. But you'll also want to find God's will for ways to serve him even before you know the answers to these questions.

If you have been asking God to reveal his will regarding your career or your future mate, we believe that if God appeared to you, he would give you a great big hug and offer words of reassurance. He might say, "My child, my child, there are thousands of believers you could marry who would be equally right for you, and there are thousands of different jobs that would allow you to be a positive influence for me. I am more concerned with your character than your job title. As you choose a career and a mate, I will be there to help you—if you listen to me. But don't worry if you make some major blunders along the way. I will still love you and help you grow even from those mistakes."

Sometimes God does have a specific mate or career in mind for his followers. But he operates in unique ways with all of us. I (Dr. Meier) was at the funeral of fellow Trinity professor Paul Little in 1976. Billy Graham's brother-in-law Leighton Ford gave the eulogy and talked about the many ways Paul Little had been a pioneer for Christ. Then he asked the audience this question, "When you are old and look back on your life, what will you see that shows you were a pioneer for Christ?" As I listened, I immediately knew God wanted me to leave the security of Trinity Seminary, which I loved, and teach counseling at Dallas Theological Seminary, where they had no counseling program.

In this case, God did have a specific job in mind for me. In other cases, he wants us to decide for ourselves, using the boundaries he has provided in Scripture. God wants us to seek His will every day as we go through life, in both specific decisions and moral decisions.

As psychiatrists, we know that most people decide which sins they want to commit, and then find a religion to back up their decisions. Sincerely seeking God's will may result in your looking for a new church, and it definitely will lead you to attend one if you are not currently attending one (see Hebrews 10:24-25).

Harbor Lights

Most people are afraid God will call them to leave their friends and family and be an overseas missionary. He does call some to do this, but when he does, he also places the desire in their hearts. You can be sure that God will use you for something that interests you and that fits your talents and abilities. He's not as concerned about *what* you do as *how* you do it.

Many people try to decide what they are going to do with their lives without ever asking for God's guidance. Then once they decide, they ask God to bless their plans. We call that "baptizing" your decision. When you do this, you are probably settling for second best. Rather than placing your faith in God and trusting in his goodness, you have limited him by perceiving him as simply a genie in a bottle.

When you come to what we call crossroads decisions, how do you know what to do? Clarence Wagner, the former CEO of Bridges for Peace, an organization that helps build relationships between Christians and

Jews internationally, uses God's "Harbor Lights of Guidance." Apparently, there is a port in Italy that is impossible to maneuver at night. The channel is so narrow and the rocks so jagged that anyone who attempts to cross risks certain shipwreck. In order to guide the ships in safely, port authorities have strategically placed three beacons of light at certain points, and if the ship's pilot lines up the lights so that they appear as one light, then he knows he is in the channel and can safely enter. However, if the pilot sees two lights, or even three lights, he knows disaster will surely follow.

When seeking God's will, make sure these three "harbor lights" line up:

> Does the decision align with God's Word?
> Do you sense God's purpose for you?
> Is the time right? Are the circumstances in line?

Does the decision align with God's Word?

God is not going to call you to become a prostitute or a bank robber.

We've all heard of people with mental illness who have murdered their children or hurt themselves because they believed God directed their actions. Many of our patients who have attempted suicide tell us they heard God tell them to do it. Jesus said in the last days, false prophets will deceive many people (Matthew 24:10-12).

Whenever you are attempting to discern the will of God, you must test the message. God's plan for your life will always line up with what the Bible teaches, and he encourages you to run everything through the filter of his Word.

> **Dear friends, do not believe every spirit, but test the spirits to see whether they are from God, because many false prophets have gone out into the world.**   1 JOHN 4:1

The more time we spend studying the Bible, the deeper our knowledge and understanding of God's will becomes. As our hearts and minds are transformed by his Word, so our ability to discern his purpose increases.

> **Do not conform any longer to the pattern of this world, but be transformed by the renewing of your mind. Then you will be able to test and approve what God's will is—his good, pleasing and perfect will.** ROMANS 12:2

Do you sense God's purpose for you?

Only God can tell you what your purpose is. Many parents try to persuade their children to be lawyers, doctors, or engineers. These are all good careers, but if they are not what God has for these people, they will be settling for second best. Discovering God's will is usually a matter of prayer and patience.

In the Old Testament, Gideon put out a fleece in an attempt to find God's will.

> **Gideon prayed to God, "I know that you promised to help me rescue Israel, but I need proof. Tonight I'll put some wool on the stone floor of that threshing-place over there. If you really will help me rescue Israel, then tomorrow morning let there be dew on the wool, but let the stone floor be dry." And that's just what happened.** JUDGES 6:36-38, CEV

Today, however, we have the Holy Spirit and the Bible to lead us, so believers should not need to put out fleeces in order to discern God's will.

We once knew a patient who would ask God a question, then consider the answer yes if the next airplane she saw had a trail of smoke behind it. Another patient made decisions based on which color of birds came to her bird feeder. If she saw a red bird first, the answer was yes, but if a blue bird came first, then the answer was no.

Be very careful that you aren't relying on a sign that *you* have chosen to confirm a decision. When Satan challenged Jesus to prove his deity by jumping off the temple roof, Jesus responded, "Do not put the Lord your God to the test" (Luke 4:12). You are testing God if you're trying to force him to choose between two possibilities of your own choosing.

I (Dr. Clements) once encountered a foreign physician who was losing his visitor status here in the States and was about to be sent back to his home country. He had become a Christian the week before he was supposed to leave, and those who led him to Christ wanted him to stay longer in order to disciple him and prepare him to share his faith with his friends and family at home. They even considered hiding him if necessary, but then decided to hold a prayer meeting and seek God's will instead.

The very next day a frail, elderly woman had her first appointment with this foreign doctor. She was impressed by him and asked him several personal questions. He told her about the predicament he was facing. She said, "I'll tell my son and see what he can do." The doctor thanked her for her concern but didn't think twice about her comment. He figured no matter what the son did, it would be of little help at this point.

Two days later he received word that he had been granted permission to stay in the United States. It turns out the woman's son was a high-ranking congressman, who was able to extend this doctor's visa. This story clearly shows that if God wills something, he will always make a way for it to happen.

You've probably seen events in your own life that seemed like coincidences at the time. But they might also have been God moving in your life behind the scenes to guide you.

Is the time right?

God's timing is not our timing. Sometimes we must wait on God. One morning, a preacher felt called to mission work in Africa. By noon he had resigned from his church and packed his bags. He waited several weeks for a mission agency to call him, but the phone never rang. He decided he must have heard God incorrectly and asked his church to take him back, which they did.

Several years later he was asked to go to Africa for a month to train new pastors. The African pastors loved him and asked him to stay and continue training new ministers. He spent the rest of his life in Africa doing mission work. He had heard God correctly; he had just rushed ahead without considering God's timing.

I (Dr. Meier) knew when I was sixteen that God was calling me to be a physician, but I still had to go to school and put in many hours a week before I was qualified to become a psychiatrist. I found medical school so difficult that at one point I lifted my books over my head, ready to throw them down and quit. Just then, my cadaver mate, Frank Minirth, walked by. He stopped and prayed with me, and then he said, "Paul, you only have six more months to go. If you had to wade waist high in mud for six more months to be a doctor for Christ, it would be worth it." Was it a coincidence that Frank walked in at just that moment? I don't think so.

Following God's will won't always be easy. As we saw in chapter 2, when the apostle Paul dedicated his life to Christ, his life seemed to get worse: he was shipwrecked twice, nearly stoned to death, hungry, imprisoned, and eventually died a martyr's death. Are you willing to receive all these gifts if you make Christ the Lord of your life? Don't do it unless you are.

Evangelist Henry Varley once challenged his friend D. L. Moody with these words: "The world has yet to see what God will do with a man fully consecrated to him." Are you that person?

More than a million people have trusted Christ through the various ministries of the Meier Clinics over the past thirty years. And it all started with a sixteen-year-old's dream that Leighton Ford, Dr. Bill Wilson, Dr. Frank Minirth, Dr. David Larson, and Dr. Jean-Luc Bertrand kept alive.

If God wants you to be a factory worker, be the best factory worker you can be, and be a witness of God's love while you are there. If he calls you to be a pastor, be the best pastor you can be, keeping your family as a higher priority than your ministry. And if he calls you to keep someone's dream alive, be the very best encourager you can be, knowing that dreams do come true.

Straying from the Path

Many people stray from God's path for their lives. Sometimes they wake up and get back on the path, although they will never know how many opportunities they may have missed as a result of their detour.

In the Old Testament, when the Israelites reached the Promised Land of Canaan, Moses sent twelve spies into the land to scout it out. When they returned, only Joshua and Caleb trusted God enough to go in. The other ten spies persuaded the people that doing so would be too dangerous. It was only when God killed these ten spies that the people changed their minds and wanted to go in. But then it was too late. Their children got to go in, but the entire first generation—except for Joshua and Caleb—was forced to stay in the desert for forty years. They strayed from God's will, and in doing so, they missed out on forty years of great blessing.

Of course, this was not what God originally wanted for his people. But even though they walked away from his leading, he was still with them during those forty years. He provided them with food every day and gave them shoes that never wore out.

God expects us to grow wherever we are planted. It doesn't matter if you are a broke college student or the president of the United States; he expects us all to live godly lives, and he will honor that.

On September 11, 2001, many of us were grieving the loss of our fellow Americans, fearful of what terrorists might do next. People close to George Bush say that when the strikes occurred, the president recognized that God had called him for that very day and that very hour. He prayed every day for God's guidance, and millions have prayed for George Bush every day since that time. It's been said that President Bush is often on his knees asking for God's will and that he is willing to do that will even if the elite of this world disagree with his decisions.

Are you willing to do God's will, even if people hate you for not going down the path they may choose for you? We hope so.

The Bottom Line

God has a specific plan for every person's life. But his will may or may not include a specific job or mate or city to live in.

God wants us all to genuinely love and serve others, just like Jesus.

To know God's will, you must first know God and be willing to follow his leading. It's tempting to let our wills override God's will. But when we do this, we settle for second best in life. Wrong choices are not necessarily sinful choices, and some choices may even be in favor of good things. But if they are not God's will for you, you may discover a lack of peace or feel spiritual tension inside.

God loves you and has equipped you for his calling. Following him will surely lead you through some hard times and lesson learning to build character, but keep your focus on what he has called you to do. Going off on your own usually leads you too close to the "hot stoves" of life. If you do get off track, however, don't forget that God is always willing to take you back and use you for his Kingdom.

Jesus is like the shepherd who temporarily left the ninety-nine obedient sheep in order to retrieve the one sheep who had gone astray. Do you feel distant from God right now? If so, which one of you has moved?

CHAPTER 12

No One Likes an Adult Child

So Grow Up

*Everyone is a moon, and has a dark side
which he never shows to anybody.*

MARK TWAIN, *FOLLOWING THE EQUATOR*

✦

*Few things are harder to put up with than the
annoyance of a good example.*

MARK TWAIN, *PUDD'NHEAD WILSON*

THERE ARE MILLIONS OF adult children in America today. What does an adult child look like? Michael Jackson may be coming to your mind right now, but adult children have many different appearances. Let's examine a few.

I (Dr. Clements) saw Susan in my clinic several years ago. She said I had four months to make her feel better or she was buying a one-way ticket to England and becoming a missionary. She didn't appreciate my laughter.

As we talked, Susan poured out her problem. She said her husband was always on her case. If he did not like her hair, she would spend thirty minutes in the bathroom redoing it. Susan agonized over what to cook for dinner, because she was always worried her husband wouldn't like what she cooked. The couple made love often, although most of the time Susan did not feel up to it. She never told her husband how she felt, however, because she did not want to upset him.

Susan's mother complained that Susan was too lenient with her children, which led to their misbehavior. Susan's mother insisted Susan bring her daughters over to visit every Saturday afternoon. Susan often did not feel like visiting, especially since her oldest daughter usually had plans of her own. But Susan went anyway and made Kari go too, so she wouldn't displease her mother.

Susan claimed she could never please her friends either. They often commented that Susan would look better if she lost ten to fifteen pounds. Susan felt guilty because her girlfriends thought her wardrobe needed updating, but she didn't have the money for new clothes. She was afraid her friends might not want to go places with her if she didn't dress more fashionably.

Susan admitted she still felt like a little girl sometimes and hated that feeling. She had recently heard a missionary from Great Britain talk about the need for more missionaries in that country. She thought her unhappiness might be a sign that God wanted to push her somewhere else—maybe England—where he could better use her. She thought I was crazy when I said her problem was that she had never grown up.

Another client, Carl, came to see me wanting medicine for depression. He said that a doctor had diagnosed him with a melancholy personality type due to his artistic nature, which left him susceptible to prolonged moods of depression. Carl also frequently smoked marijuana to relieve his anxiety and melancholic personality.

When Carl was nine years old, he cut his hand playing with his father's electric saw, and though doctors tried to save it, his hand was amputated. His parents, especially his father, felt guilty and blamed themselves for his accident. Carl had learned to live a relatively normal life with only one hand. In fact, he learned to write and perform other activities very well with his remaining hand.

He expressed his self-proclaimed artistic nature by singing in a rock band with three other immature twentysomethings (and I use the word *singing* very loosely). The group played the local nightclubs every once in a while. Carl didn't need a job because his parents supported him, so he spent his time playing around or working on his band. He was under the delusion that his garage band was on the way to stardom. His parents felt they owed him this chance, since his injured hand had held him back in other activities. Therefore, Carl was relieved of any responsibility in his life.

Carl's irresponsibility permeated almost every area of his life and had begun to worry his parents. When Carl missed an appointment with me, his mother would call to reschedule. She became angry when I told her that only Carl could reschedule an appointment. Carl's parents scheduled a meeting with me (with Carl's permission) to discuss how I might help Carl become more responsible and plan for the future. If his band didn't make it big (and after listening to their music I can assure you they won't), Carl planned to help disabled kids like himself. This was a worthwhile goal, but Carl had absolutely no idea how to go about reaching it.

Like Susan, Carl's problem was that he had never grown up. His parents thought I was crazy when I suggested Carl was an adult child and they were the ones enabling him. His father looked me in the eye and said, "How can you say that when we're offering him every opportunity to make something of himself?"

"Well, if my parents paid for every want in my life, I wouldn't have a job either," I responded.

Even though Carl's handicap was minimal, he continued to play the disability trump card with his parents. He and I talked quite openly about this. I knew a job would have benefited him tremendously, giving him self-confidence, a sense of accomplishment, and a feeling of responsibility. But why should he get a job if he didn't have to?

Carl stopped seeing me because I wouldn't give him stimulants for his "melancholic personality." Two years later, his parents came back to see me. Carl was now in his thirties, and they were still supporting him. Only now, they were also supporting his wife and baby as well. His mother realized that my initial assessment had been correct and wanted to know what they should do. My answer was still the same—cut his money off and he would learn responsibility rather than starve. His father said they just couldn't do that because there was a child involved now. Sadly, Carl will likely never have to become a true adult.

I saw another adult child, Kyle, at his sister's request because he had a terrible temper. His first question was, "Hey, Doc, have you got a pill that could help my temper?" This is like saying, "I've got a problem with cussing. Rather than learning to hold my tongue, I want a pill that will stop me."

Kyle had graduated from college two years earlier with a business degree and a 4.0 grade point average. He was a go-getter, and everyone expected him to climb the corporate ladder very quickly. But Kyle's rise had been stymied by arguments with coworkers. Kyle was a hard worker and had great ideas, but if anybody criticized or suggested a correction to his work, Kyle unleashed his wrath. He felt that his higher grade point average and degree from a tough business school made him superior to those he worked with. His attitude earned him a pink slip.

And the trouble didn't stop at work. Kyle also lost several girlfriends because of his arrogance and condescending attitude. His most recent breakup was particularly troubling. He and Emily were engaged with a wedding date six months away, until she told some friends at a party about Kyle's recent speeding ticket. Kyle, furious that she had embarrassed him, screamed at Emily until she tearfully called off the wedding. Kyle did eventually apologize to Emily, but it was too late to repair the damage.

Kyle agreed that his actions were not worth the grief they had caused him, but he did admit that if he were in those same situations again, his responses would be the same. He was so adamant that nobody was going to take advantage of him, he sabotaged his own success.

Kyle's parents had been very demanding and harsh with him when he was growing up, and he built up a tremendous resentment toward them. He decided that now that he was an adult, no one would ever make him feel like a child again. Ironically, he acted just like a kid whenever life did not go his way.

Susan, Carl, and Kyle were all legal adults, but functionally they were still children. Susan could not stand up for herself and make her own decisions due to feelings of inferiority. Carl could not face up to the responsibilities of adulthood. Kyle could make decisions and handle responsibility, but he refused to deal with others or their opinions. These are all lessons that should have been successfully mastered during adolescence.

Understanding Adolescence

We all entered life as helpless children. We totally depended on adults for food, clothing, and shelter. Adults made our decisions: when we went to bed, got up, went to school, ate dinner, etc. This is called the one-down position. Children are lower in position than adults—all adults.

This begins to change during the period of adolescence. Children are gradually given more and more responsibility over their lives. They begin deciding when to go to bed, who to hang out with, what classes to take in school, what extracurricular activities they want to participate in, and so on. As these skills are mastered, greater freedoms are granted—driving, dating, working a job, and spending self-made money.

Late adolescence marks the transition into adulthood, and after high school graduation many teens move out and start practicing life as adults. I (Dr. Meier) told our six teenagers that as soon as they graduated from high school, they had three months to move out and support themselves unless they attended college at least twelve credits a semester and maintained at least a C average. One of our teens graduated from high school early and wasn't quite mature enough to handle college away from home at age seventeen. After quitting college and moving into a tent with some other teens at a camping park in California, our teen called to complain of hunger and asked me to wire money immediately for food.

I am actually a big teddy bear with a soft heart, but I knew if I enabled our teen, I would be hurting more than helping, so I said I would not send money. I said that the only way to avoid starvation was to take the first available job and buy food with the first paycheck. So our teen got the only job that paid cash on the spot—shoveling manure out of the outhouses at the park where they were camping. After two weeks of shoveling manure, our teen was ready to buckle down and go back to college with real motivation. After seven years of earning straight A's, my child later received a $250,000 scholarship and went on to get two PhDs. It is amazing what a little manure will do for you.

During late adolescence, teens also learn they are no longer in a one-down position to adults; they are equal with adults. But this freedom of equality also brings responsibility. Adults make their own decisions without permission from others. They choose their own opinions and set their own values. True adults don't have to gain acceptance and approval from others in order to feel okay about themselves.

Many important decisions are made during later adolescence: Whom will I marry? What will my career be? Where will I live? Ninety percent of people decide what religion—if any—they will follow during their teenage years. Life virtues are also set in place during this time—honesty, generosity, morality, and character. It is imperative that an adolescent learns to make her own decisions, or the rest of her life could consist of choices others have made for her. Living a life full of other peoples' choices affects most people exactly like it did Susan—it extinguishes hope and freedom, ushering in depression and despair.

Adolescents must navigate this sometimes-tricky road to becoming an adult, and parents can be the best "ace in the hole" a teenager has. The astute parent realizes when it is time for a child to leave the nest and starts helping the adolescent to fly (much like an eagle teaches her young to fly, although adolescents take years to launch, not days). The parent's exact role will differ according to each adolescent.

Some parents have to push forward and some have to pull back. My (Dr. Clements) wife says she knew exactly what she wanted out of life at a young age and can remember longing to be grown up. Her parents gave her some freedom but did hold her back a little until she was ready to fly on her own. Other parents have to push, encouraging their children to have more freedoms, take on more responsibility, and form mature relationships with other young adults.

Parents can retard this growth (even unknowingly), causing harm in their child's maturing process. I (Dr. Clements) used to be a college campus minister. In that position, I knew a number of college students who still lived at home. In a few instances, the parents still treated the students like they were in high school, which was very damaging to them.

One such student, Steven, very much wanted to come to our freshmen Bible study. It would have been a great opportunity for him to make new friends (as most of his friends had gone to college elsewhere) and get involved in college life. But the freshmen groups met on Monday night at seven o'clock, which was the night Steven's grandmother joined the family for dinner. Steven was expected to pick her up from the retirement home and return her after dinner.

I suggested that Steven inform his parents of his desire to attend Bible study and ask either to be excused from Monday night dinner or have Grandma on another night. They refused. I felt bad that Steven was left out of the Bible studies and other fun activities as well.

I've seen other college students whose parents forced them to come home on weekends. One student's mother, who lived about an hour from the college campus, expected him to drive home every Friday afternoon and work his high school job at the local grocery store. When he tried to tell his mother he could work in his college town, she became angry. She tried to make him feel guilty by reminding him that the local grocery store owner desperately needed someone responsible on the weekends.

Another way parents can produce adult children is to constantly bail their kids out of problems. Remember Carl from our earlier example? Although his mother and father meant well, their actions backfired. They were trying to pave the way for him to be a successful, fully functioning adult, but in the process, they taught Carl to always take the path of least resistance.

Success seldom comes without struggle. Birds are a prime example of this. Mother birds (and father birds in some species) sit on their eggs, keeping them protected and warm until it's time to hatch. The mother bird then leaves the nest, and the baby bird must break through the egg on its own. It pecks and pecks, rolling around in the egg and looking as if it's in desperate pain, as it tries to escape the tiny round cage.

It is difficult to watch a baby bird struggle while hatching and not reach out to help. In fact many people with good intentions do crack the egg in an attempt to help the baby bird escape without any further struggle. But this ultimately results in the baby bird's death. You see, the baby bird must struggle in order to build its muscles and harden its beak enough to make it in the real world. What was meant for good turns out to be disastrous.

The hardest thing for a parent to do is watch a child fail and suffer. It's tempting to help a child up and say, "Now go forth and learn from that mistake." But if there are no consequences from the mistake, there is also little learning. Someone who experiences no ramifications from failure often has little desire to succeed. People need to fail, and they need to experience the pain from that failure. This is what drives them to try harder or try something different the next time.

Carl couldn't have cared less about succeeding because his parents had him set up so he couldn't fail. It's true that Carl suffered an unfortunate accident. But remember what we learned in chapter 2? Life is not fair.

Our society seems to encourage people to remain children rather than become adults. During my (Dr. Clements) residency training, I worked in an evening psychiatry clinic that performed disability evaluations. What I saw there still makes me sick to my stomach. People came through our doors in droves, hoping to be diagnosed with any kind of psychiatric problem so they could get a disability check from the government and not have to work. They would move from doctor to doctor until they finally found someone to put them on disability.

I also saw patients who were already on disability. Most of them had become depressed after receiving this assistance. They had no purpose, nowhere to be, no one who needed them, and nothing meaningful to do.

Of course some people do need and deserve disability, but the problem with the system is that it erases the hope of true success. Disability guarantees a recipient will never totally fail (because he gets a small check each month—usually at the poverty level) but will never succeed either. This can be enormously demoralizing.

A 2005 survey revealed that the vast majority of people who "internalize" are chronically happy and content, while those who "externalize" are chronically depressed and miserable. When an internalizer runs out of money, he gets an extra job or does whatever it takes to care for himself. If he feels lonely, he calls a friend. If he is sad, he grieves and gets over it. Internalizers assume responsibility for their own lives, their own emotions, and their own financial and other needs.

According to the survey, externalizers continually look outside themselves for help, are constantly disappointed, and always feel like victims of society. If externalizers are broke, they seek handouts from the government or their families. If they are lonely, they get angry at whoever they believe is neglecting them. If they have unmet emotional needs, they blame their spouses or others for not meeting their needs. Externalizers are usually filled with self-pity and bitterness.

Jim Stovall's Story

Raised in Tulsa, Oklahoma, Jim Stovall was a bright kid who matured into a promising teenager. On his eighteenth birthday he had the whole world in his hands.

He was the national champion in Olympic-style weight lifting for his age and weight division and was training for the 1980 Olympic Games when his world changed forever. During a routine physical, the physician called in several of his physician colleagues, and each took a turn looking in Jim's eyes. Every time, Jim asked what was happening, but he got no answers. Finally, one of the doctors broke the news that Jim had a rare eye disease that would progressively worsen until he was completely blind.

At first, Jim refused to believe the news, but the doctors were right, and his eyesight gradually diminished until he could no longer deny it was happening. By the time he was twenty-eight, Jim was completely blind.

He settled into a small room in the back of his house, resigned to the fact that he would have to spend the rest of his life right there. He tried to "watch" some of the movies from his extensive collection, but he was quickly frustrated because unless someone was speaking in a scene, he had no idea what was going on. He kept thinking that someone should create a television station that narrated action for those who were blind.

During the next several years, people laughed at Jim's idea. Television producers told him it would never work, and he had little money to start his venture. But Jim never gave up. At first Jim narrated the movies himself, but eventually he convinced the stars of these movies to record interviews with him. The biggest movie stars of that day, including Katharine Hepburn, Michael Douglas, Eddie Albert, Peter Graves, and Frank Sinatra, agreed to be interviewed. He started with one cable television station in Tulsa, Oklahoma, and today Narrative Television Network (NTN) is carried on several thousand stations as well as the Internet at www.NarrativeTV.com.

Jim didn't stop there. He became a best-selling author with books like *You Don't Have to Be Blind to See* and *The Ultimate Gift*. These books have been printed in numerous languages around the world, and in 2006, *The Ultimate Gift* was made into a film.

Today he is one of the most well-known and sought after motivational speakers in this country. Jim has done so many wonderful things, we don't have room to name them all in this book. What was his secret?

He says he changed his mind, which changed his life. He could have sat around feeling sorry for himself and spent the rest of his life being angry at God. At first, he was externalizing—bitter, blaming God, blaming others, and not realizing the potential he had to do something great. Then he began to internalize, realizing that he couldn't change what had happened to him, but he could make the world a better place. He has certainly done that.

You can do that too! But you must first become an adult and take responsibility for your life. We all have something to overcome. The harder your barrier is to overcome, the sweeter your success will be when you do. In reality, the world owes no one anything, and those who feel that it does are always disappointed and unsatisfied.

This world is filled with unhappy, unfulfilled, and bitter people who spend each day wasting the many opportunities they have to make life better for themselves and others around them. They blame their discontent on everyone else, and if they can't find a human, they blame God. They look externally, or horizontally, for happiness. They count on other people, money, circumstances, or pleasure to fulfill. And when it doesn't happen, bitterness and self-pity set in.

Real Life as a Real Adult

My (Dr. Clements) mother ate healthy food, exercised, and never smoked, but she battled two cases of breast cancer in her forties. Chemotherapy and radiation were hard on her, especially when she had to wear a wig to my brother's wedding because all of her hair had fallen out. She found out later that she has a rare cancer gene and had to undergo even more surgery. Doctors have told her that even with everything they have done, there is a good chance she will develop cancer again somewhere in her body. Does she sit around and complain to God how unfair life is? Does she feel cheated because she lived a healthy life and might die of cancer at a younger age than most? Nope.

She got involved in Reach to Recovery, and today the doctors often call her when they have a newly diagnosed cancer patient who needs support. She devotes several hours each week to serving these women: counseling them, educating them, praying with them, linking them with support groups, and preparing them for what will happen next. Most of these women are scared and don't know what to do. Through this volunteer effort, my mother has talked to lawmakers, governors, insurance executives, and other people who have an impact on the future of cancer research. I am very proud of my mother.

God has provided my mom with a ministry and purpose through her cancer. She says she used to dread the day my youngest brother left home because nurturing a Christian family was her primary purpose. When the time came for my little brother to leave, however, she had his bags packed and was ready for him to hit the road. She allowed God to use her "bleeding" as a blessing for others. She sometimes says she wonders whether if she had not had the cancer, she would be sitting around the house bored with life—or calling her kids three times a day.

My mother knows her cancer could return tomorrow and she could die within a month, but the same could be said for all of us. She tells stories about the way some women cannot overcome their anger and then end up with depression on top of cancer. They allow cancer to stop their joy in life.

The Bible clearly teaches that joy comes from God and not circumstances. Don't look horizontally, but instead, look vertically. Start by looking up to God, then down to your heart, and then back up into your mind. Accept God in your heart, learn about him in your mind, and find the peace, joy, and satisfaction he promises to provide within you. Once you have that, you can stop looking to others.

Children expect others to meet all of their needs. Children don't worry about the needs of others. Children are supposed to be selfish. That's why God gave them parents.

Adult children look to others to meet all their needs and don't worry about the needs of others. Adult children are selfish. But unlike real children, they are rarely happy or content with life. Many of them come to counseling to find happiness. Some will make a breakthrough when they realize that playing the role of victim results in a downward spiral to more helplessness and depression. These people can then take responsibility for and control of their lives and learn to focus on serving others rather than being served.

Others, sadly, never see past their role as helpless victims. Counseling becomes just one more opportunity to have a captive audience to garner sympathy. When the sympathy runs out, they start looking for the next counselor.

Adult children complain that if other people would only change, then they would be happier. True adults realize that changing from within is the only way to find happiness. Adult children ask God to change others to suit them. True adults ask God to change them to better suit him. Adult children wake up in the morning and give God a to-do list for the day, and then they go to bed bitter that he didn't do what he was told to do. True adults get up in the morning and ask God what they can do for him.

Abraham Lincoln once said, "Most people are about as happy as they make up their minds to be." As psychiatrists, we see people who inherit depression but live "happily ever after" on corrective medications. But we also see people who are almost begging for depression. These people need a radical attitude shift. Philippians 4:13 is one of our favorite verses, and it always hangs in Dr. Meier's office:

> **I can do all things through Christ who strengthens me.** NKJV

We can't do it alone, and he won't do it for us. But we can do whatever needs to be done with his wisdom and his strength. The Bible is an internalizing book from cover to cover.

The Bottom Line

True adults leave this world better than they found it. They serve others in order to show the love of God.

Adult children take from this world all they can grab. They expect others to serve them and believe others should give to them freely. The book of Proverbs describes adult children very well. It refers to them as fools. There's no guarantee of earthly success for the true adult, but there is a 100 percent guarantee of failure for adult children. Which one are you going to be? The answer to this question will make all the difference in your life. This question is answered by actions—not words.

I (Dr. Clements) want to leave you with one last word of wisdom from a very dear person, my mother, Lou Anne Clements. My mother taught me how to love God, even though I don't always understand his infinite wisdom, and to love and serve others even when they let me down. She taught me to accept myself enough to allow God to use me, while practicing patience as he changes me.

Most people hear very little of what you say because your actions are too loud.

One Final Question:
What Have You Learned?

If you've learned any lessons since you "knew it all," we'd love to hear about them. We hope to use them in our follow-up book, which will feature a section allowing you and other readers to tell your true stories.

Please type up your story in five hundred words or less and suggest a title. Include any Scripture passages that support your story or have been particularly meaningful to you. Provide us with your contact information (preferably both an e-mail and a street address). If we decide to use it, we will let you know.

You can submit your story at www.drtoddclements.com.

We look forward to hearing from you.

Sincerely,
Todd Clements, M.D.
Paul Meier, M.D.

PAUL MEIER, M.D.

Dr. Paul Meier is a nationally recognized psychiatrist and founder of the Meier Clinics, a national chain of counseling and day-program facilities that employ 140 psychiatrists, psychologists, and therapists.

Dr. Meier has authored and coauthored more than seventy books, including *Love Is a Choice, Happiness Is a Choice, Winning Is a Choice, Unbreakable Bonds,* and *Blue Genes.* He has hosted a live national talk radio program for twenty years and is a frequent guest on numerous radio and television programs, including *The Oprah Winfrey Show* and Joyce Meyer's *Enjoying Everyday Life.* In addition, he has been interviewed on Radio Free Europe and has appeared in a French television documentary discussing Christian psychiatry.

Acknowledged as a pioneer in the integration of psychological and spiritual dimensions with physical aspects, Dr. Meier has taught at many universities and seminaries throughout the world. A well-known national and international speaker, he lectures on insight-oriented therapy and other related topics. Dr. Meier has been a guest speaker for the past three years at Awakening, an annual weekend retreat for business and political leaders to exchange ideas, examine trends, and learn from leading authorities and policy makers in a variety of fields.

Dr. Meier also served as a member of the Dallas Mayor and Dallas County Judge's Health Alliance.

Dr. Meier received his master's degree in cardiovascular physiology from Michigan State University and a medical degree from the University of Arkansas College of Medicine in Little Rock. He completed his psychiatry residency at Duke University Medical Center. In 1984, he obtained another degree from Dallas Theological Seminary.

In addition to his busy speaking and writing schedule, Dr. Meier treats patients at the Meier Clinics Day Program in Richardson, Texas.

TODD M. CLEMENTS, M.D.

Dr. Clements served as a youth pastor and motivational speaker during college. Upon graduation, he pursued a master's degree in divinity from Southwestern Baptist Theological Seminary in Fort Worth, Texas, in preparation for a career in the ministry. The Lord had different plans, however, leading him to pursue a career in medicine.

Dr. Clements obtained his medical degree from the University of Arkansas. He served as president of his class all four years of medical school. He then completed his residency training in psychiatry at the University of Oklahoma–Tulsa, where he served as chief resident of the program.

Dr. Clements began his career in psychiatry with the Paul Meier Clinics in Dallas, Texas. While there, he founded "Breakaway," an intensive counseling program designed specifically for teenagers. Dr. Clements also coauthored the book *Blue Genes* with Dr. Meier.

Today Dr. Clements is a board certified adolescent and adult psychiatrist with the Amen Clinics. He specializes in SPECT Brain Imaging, a nuclear medicine study that is on the cutting edge of psychiatry. Dr. Clements and his colleagues at the Amen Clinics are using SPECT imaging with their patients in order to better diagnose and treat mental health issues.

Dr. Clements is a columnist for *Maximum Fitness* magazine and a sought-after speaker. He lives in Newport Beach, California, with Lynda, his wife of ten years.

We would like to thank Lisa Jackson and Liz Duckworth

for the hours of work they spent applying their

fantastic editing skills to this book.

NOTES

1. www.cdc.gov/nchs/fastats/divorce.htm
2. www.marriagealliance.org/id41.htm
3. www.divorcereform.org
4. Lorrain Ali and Lisa Miller, "The Secret Lives of Wives," *Newsweek*, July 12, 2004, http://www.newsweek.com/id/54389.
5. Darryl S. Inaba and William E. Cohen, *Uppers, Downers, All Arounders* (Ashland, OR: CNS Publications, Inc., 2004), 170.
6. Ibid., 244.
7. Ibid., 91–92.
8. British National Treatment Agency for Abuse, 2004 Report. www.nta.nhs.uk.
9. Ed Vitagliano, "Porn Profits Surge on Main Street," AgapePress, December 5, 2006, http://headlines.agapepress.org/archive/12/52006c.asp.
10. National Center for Health Statistics, "Prevalence of Overweight and Obesity Among Adults: United States, 2003–2004," Centers for Disease Control and Prevention, http://www.cdc.gov/nchs/products/pubs/pubd/hestats/overweight/overwght_adult_03.htm.
11. www.aweighout.com